A Near-Death Researcher's Notebook

What I Have Learned About Dying, Death, and the Afterlife

Kenneth Ring

A Near-Death Researcher's Notebook: What I Have Learned About Dying, Death, and the Afterlife

Published by Wheatmark®
2030 East Speedway Boulevard, Suite 106
Tucson, Arizona 85719 USA
www.wheatmark.com

ISBN: 979-8-88747-033-7
LCCN: 2023900063

Bulk ordering discounts are available through Wheatmark, Inc.
For more information, email orders@wheatmark.com or call 1-888-934-0888.

Contents

Facing Death

End of Life Revelations

Introduction

After publishing five books dealing with near-death experiences (NDEs), ending with the turn of the millennium, I continued to write, just on other subjects. But eventually I was compelled to give up writing books altogether, so in recent years I've taken up the blogging life. However, once I had written quite a few blogs, I figured that if I just rebranded them as "essays," I could collect them into books of essays. And so I did.

In the last few years, I've published three such books, *Waiting to Die*, *Reflections in a Glass Eye* and *Blogging Toward Infinity*. The first book sold surprisingly well, but the last two were flops. I just licked my wounds, staunched my disappointment and figured that would be the end of my writing life.

But not quite, as you see.

It occurred to me that since I had written quite a few essays, not only on NDEs, but on issues related to death and dying as well, that I could gather up these scattered essays, tie them up with a pretty bow and ribbon, and bring them out in a new book for readers interested in the recent writing I've done on such subjects since many people did not avail themselves of my previous two books.

So in a way, this is a kind of summing up of the work that has engaged me for more than the past forty years. These essays reflect not only what I've learned during this time, but what I think is most important for people to know about NDEs and death and dying.

It's better than you think, and as one of the authors I write about says, it's "nothing to be frightened of." On the contrary, these essays will show that death is not a dead end and is actually something to look forward to. Read on, and you'll see what I mean.

Starting Out

Researching Life After Life

The other night, when I was reorganizing some of my books and papers, I happened to come upon an old newsletter from forty years ago that had been edited by some then friends of mine. At the time they lived just a few miles from where I now reside, and seeing that newsletter brought back warm memories of our friendship.

But what struck me most forcibly was a little essay I had written for their publication, which was sent only to the people who were members of their organization, probably something like fifty and surely not more than a hundred. I had completely forgotten about this essay, and obviously only a relatively few people had read it at the time.

When I wrote it, I had just completed the research for my first book on NDEs, *Life at Death*. I was then deeply affected by the interviews I had conducted for the book, and in the essay I wrote about it in a very personal way. I could never, and never would, have written about my research this way in my book, but here I was still in the emotional throes of my interviews and how they had already changed my life.

I was also aware that my work had completely validated that of Raymond Moody, and for that reason, I had actually entitled my essay, *Researching "Life After Life": Some Personal Reflections."* Now in retrospect, I find something else I hadn't been so much aware of at the time — my indebtedness to Moody's book, *Life After Life*. What if I had never come across his book? How would my life have developed without that book?? Was there ever a book that was so crucial to my life's path? So, in a very definite way, if only in hindsight, I would like this essay to be read as a kind of homage to Dr. Moody and the critical role that he and his book have played in my life.

But here's what I wrote forty years ago, when I was just at the beginning of my own journey into the world of NDEs.

Beginning in May of 1977, I spent thirteen months tracking down and interviewing persons who had come close to death. In some cases, these were persons who appeared to have suffered clinical death where there is no heartbeat or respiration; in most cases, however, the individuals I talked with had "merely" edged toward the brink of death but did not quite slip over.

Since this work was part of a research project, I had trained a staff of interviewers in the necessary procedures so that I – the busy professor – would not have to conduct all the interviews myself. After I had talked with a couple of near-death survivors, though, I saw that my life would just have to get busier: this stuff was plainly too fascinating to get it secondhand. I wound up interviewing 74 of the 102 persons who eventually comprised our sample.

Although I had been familiar with near-death experiences for some years, my interest in doing research in the area had been kindled by Raymond Moody's book, *Life After Life.* I found that, although I didn't really question the basic paradigm that he described, I was left with a lot of questions after finishing the book. How frequent were these experiences? Did it make any difference *how* one (almost) died? For example, do suicide attempts that bring one close to death engender the typical near-death experience? What role does prior religiousness play in shaping the experience? Can the changes that allegedly follow from these experiences be documented systematically and quantitatively?

So I wrote a little grant proposal and got some funds in order to answer these questions.

And thereby uncovered a source of spiritual wealth that will always sustain me.

This was not exactly what I had bargained for. But I am happy to "share the wealth" with you. Not that it's mine or was given to me. Nor does it "belong" to those who survive near-death episodes. It's just there. It's simply that talking to these persons helped me to *see* it.

In this little article, I am not going to bother to summarize the results from this study except to say that our data fully uphold Moody's findings. Virtually every aspect of the near-death experience he delineated is to be found in our interview protocols. I have no doubt whatever that he has described an authentic phenomenon (though its interpretation is up for grabs). And others, since the publication of Moody's book, have also corroborated his findings. As far as I'm concerned, then, the basic outline of the core near-death experience, as sketched by Moody (and before him by Kübler-Ross) is now established fact.

What I want to relate to you is something of the experiential residue that has remained with me now that the interviews are finished. I doubt that much of this is going to find its way into the professional publications I shall be writing based on this research or that it will even find explicit expression in a book I am planning on near-death experiences. And yet, in some way, I feel that it represents the essential *finding* of my research: that it is "the real message" hidden within the welter of statistics and the seemingly endless interview excerpts which so far make up the bulk of the manuscript I am presently working on.

You don't forget their faces or their manner during the interview. I talked to one woman who had been close to death perhaps eight or nine times owing to an unusual respiratory problem. Once, when her life was in danger, she saw a ball of light and heard what she took to be the voice of the Lord. The voice said, "You will suffer, but the Kingdom of heaven will be yours." This woman insisted that these were the exact words, nor a paraphrase or "an impression." As with so many other incidents that were disclosed to me, this one seemed fully real. People will deny indignantly that what they experienced was a dream or a hallucination. But what I remember most vividly from this interview is how this woman *looked.* She radiated peace, serenity, acceptance. She knew she didn't have long to live – that the next time could be "it." She has had many personal difficulties to contend with in her life. She lives every day as a *gift.* This was not said as an empty religious platitude. I could *see* it. She never said so, but it became clear that her friends are deeply inspired by her example. (She herself makes light of it all.) I looked at her face as she continued talking. It seemed lit up – from the inside.

How do you think I felt when I left her house?

I remember another woman. She had had her near-death experience more than twenty years ago. (Most of those we interviewed had come close to death within the past two years.) Her doctor had botched up a routine tonsillectomy and a cardiac arrest had resulted. According to the information she gave me and from what I could glean from her medical records, it appears that she was clinically dead for nearly three minutes. I'll relate just a portion of what she told me:

> *...the thing I could never – absolutely <u>never</u> – forget is that <u>absolute</u> feeling of [struggling for words] peace ... joy ... or something. Because I remember the <u>feeling.</u> I just remember this <u>absolutely beautiful feeling.</u> Of peace. And happy! Oh, so happy! That's about the only way I can explain it. And I was above. And there was a presence. It's the only way I can explain it because I didn't <u>see</u> anything. But there was a <u>presence,</u> and it may not have been <u>talking</u> to me, but it was like I knew what was going on between our minds. I wanted to go that way [toward the presence]. <u>Something</u> was there. And I had no fear of it. And the <u>peace,</u> the release. The fear was all gone. There was no pain, there was nothing. It was <u>absolutely beautiful!</u> I could <u>never</u> explain it in a million years. It was a feeling that I think everyone <u>dreams</u> of someday having. Reaching a point of ABSOLUTE peace. And ever since then I've never been afraid of death.*

The woman who told me all this (and much more!) is now in her mid-fifties and had recently suffered a near-fatal heart attack. There was nothing about her manner that suggested she was denying the fear of death that Ernest Becker says each of us carries within us. I wish he could have met this woman! No reaction-formation here! I have seen her socially several times since. She is the same woman. Love of life and of others animates her. Well, maybe she was always like this, but she denies it. She traces this attitude to the time when she was "dead."

Suppose you had interviewed her. Suppose you had interviewed *dozens* of persons who described to you similar feelings, experiences and aftereffects. What impressions do you think you'd be left with as you drove back to the university?

Another person who made a deep impact on me was a husky-voiced, elegant woman in her late forties. At the time of my interview with her, she lived in a tasteful, well-appointed home in a well-to-do suburb of Hartford. The outward comfort of her life was in sharp contrast, however, to her years of severe physical suffering and psychological torment. Two years before I met her, she had lain, alone and comatose, in her home for three days before she was discovered and brought to a hospital. She had apparently suffered heart failure and lay close to death for a long time. This extended period during which she hovered between life and death enabled her to have a very deep experience, perhaps the deepest of any I heard recounted. She eventually found herself surrounded by a radiant light, feeling totally peaceful and ecstatic, reunited with her deceased parents, and in an environment which can only be described as representing a vista of what most people would call heaven. At the height of her joy, however, she felt herself being pulled back by the appeals of her children who stood around her bed, and at this point remembers experiencing an agonizingly painful wrenching sensation, as though, she said, "I was being pulled out of a *tremendous vacuum* and just being torn to bits."

Before her return to life she remembers thinking:

One very, very strong feeling was that if I could <u>only</u> make them (her doctors and others) understand how comfortable and how <u>painless</u> it is, how <u>natural</u> it is. And the feeling that I had when this was happening was not that I was becoming non-existent, but that I was becoming just another identity, another part of me was being born. I don't feel that it was an ending of my personality or my being. I just felt it was another beginning of my being. I felt <u>no</u> sadness. No longing. No fear.

Even when she was feeling the pain of being caught between the worlds, her resolve did not ebb:

I cannot tell you exactly <u>what</u> happened – whether I heard my daughter or my children speak to me, and when they said, "we need you!" (But) suddenly, the immensity of what I had experienced somehow made me realize that I <u>had</u> to, I <u>have</u> to make people understand. I have to make them realize that death is not a frightening or horrible end. <u>It is not</u>. I <u>know</u> it is not! It's just an extension or another beginning.

Since the time of this incident, this woman has been attempting to share her experiences with others. She has spoken to journalists, radio reporters, and was even in a documentary film that dealt with the experiences of dying. To live in accordance with what her near-death experience disclosed has become her life's aim. At the present writing, this woman is undertaking a program to counsel the dying and the sick. She has found her life's work and she found it through encountering her own death.

She is not the only person I talked with whose experiences have led to a mode of life devoted to helping others deal with their own deaths. Such persons who have had a near-death experience come to engage in this work not simply out of a desire to do something useful or kind, but from an inner conviction that their own experience, by virtue of its having been vouchsafed to them, is *meant* to be shared so as to provide comfort and reassurance to those who are about to take their own journeys into something that we call death. And there is something about such people I have noticed, some special quality they have that draws you to them. They seem to radiate in life the peace that they felt when they were close to death. And it *does* something to you.

I could mention many other persons I talked with who have this ability to make a gift of their presence, but I think I'll relate just one more vignette. Again, it is a woman (I think I should say that I found no sex differences in incidents of near-death experiences and many men gave me deeply affecting accounts of their episodes; it just happens that the memories that come first to mind in connection with this article all involve women), but this time it is a woman who had no conscious, Moody-type experience. In fact, though she never read Moody's books, what she had heard about such purported experiences had left her feeling skeptical in the extreme.

I had driven a long way through a dreary rain to get to her home and when I rang the doorbell, there was no response. I was about to ring again when the door finally opened. A middle-aged woman, her face showing the pain which still affected her body, silently invited me inside. I understood immediately on seeing her that she could only move slowly and with difficulty. That explained the long delay on her doorstep. She lived alone. Her husband had died some years before. Her daughters, whose photographs were displayed on the living room wall, lived in nearby towns. I noticed that her daughters were strikingly beautiful. Her house was small, but tastefully furnished. Charming knickknacks and lovely flower filled-vases gave the living room a homey and cozy quality.

She sank heavily into a chair. Speaking slowly and with a German accent, she told me that a year and a half earlier, she had been severely injured in an automobile accident of which she remembers nothing. They didn't think she would live. She showed me photographs taken at the time; they were not pretty. She spoke matter-of-factly, without any sense of self-pity. She was still recovering and she was still suffering physically, but somehow she exuded a quality of repose and serene pensiveness. She began to reflect on what her experiences had taught her:

> *In my opinion, there are two things in life which keep a person going, or, I should say, which are important. To me, they are the most important things. And that is <u>love</u> and <u>knowledge</u>. And what I experienced when I was in intensive care, not only once but several times, when I went out of my consciousness, was the closeness of another human being, the love I was treated with from everybody including the doctors and including the nurses and most of all, my family, my children. And I think a lot of people who are very religious or so will say they more or less experienced God, whatever God <u>I</u> believe in, right? And love was one of the things I felt (when) I was close to them. I got more of it than others. And I could <u>give</u> more of it, too. I felt very much loved and I felt that I loved everybody. I did not only tell one time that I loved my doctor and I still feel that way because they [she paused], they gave me life back again. I think that this is worthwhile, to love somebody, because life is the most precious thing. And I think you don't realize that before you actually almost die. (And) the more knowledge you have the better you will understand whenever anything happens to you. You will understand why certain things have to be this way and why.*
>
> *For example, a friend who was on a dying list, too, but he never believed in doctors, in nurses or anything like that. And he is <u>still</u> ill, and this is over a year now and he's still ill, very ill. Because he did not <u>trust</u> in the people, that they can help. And [she paused again] I think that's very important that you <u>know</u> that certain people love you and not only certain people, but <u>most</u> people love other people ... There may be some people, and one hears about it, that*

they live in hatred, but I think they don't have the knowledge that it is <u>so important to love</u> and to understand what life is all about because I think that's the main thing ... that's what it is all about.

I asked her if she had felt that way before her accident:

I did, but I did not feel as strong as I do now. The accident, as bad as it was and as much as I suffered and as much as I will probably never be exactly the same as I was before, but mentally I think I grew. I grew a lot. I learned the value of life more than I did before and I actually gained by this experience. It's very important to me. That itself makes life worthwhile for me to go on and do whatever is in store for me, you know, and live to the full extent.

She grew quiet then, for even talking was an effort, and I noticed the timeless stillness that had come upon us. The illumination in the room was dim, and but woman's face was again aglow with that inward light of peace and love that I had seen before in other near-death survivors. Everything in that room seemed hushed and still and suffused in beauty. Those of you who meditate or who have taken psychedelic trips will understand ... and will understand how much words fail here. Everything – all meaning, all mystery, all holiness – was present in the specificity and precision and timelessness of that moment.

With a sense of wrong-doing, I finally broke the spell by asking another question. The interview continued. At the end I tried to express my thanks to her, but lamely. She thought I was thanking her for the interview.

Afterward, still feeling immensely moved, I felt that I wanted to send her something that would better express my gratitude to her. Since she had mentioned that she enjoyed listening to music, I chose a recording of Beethoven's A minor string quartet. The third movement of this quartet is sub-titled, "Heiliger Dankgesang eines Genesenden an die Gottheit" (Hymn of Thanksgiving to the Creator from a convalescent), and in view of her accident and ancestry, it seemed fitting. This quartet also had a special personal meaning for me since I had listened to it over and over at one point in my life when I had feared (mistakenly, as it turned out) that I might be seriously ill. I thought in listening to it, she would understand.

She replied by sending me a printed card of thanks with her signature. No more. Sometime later I wrote to her in order to see whether she might be interested in appearing in a documentary film on near-death experiences, but my inquiry went unanswered. I was somehow reluctant to call her. But I have never forgotten her or what she looked like when she spoke the words I quoted to you and what happened when she had finished speaking them.

I had begun this work during a time of sorrow and inward emptiness in my life. I remember feeling spiritually adrift, as if I had somehow lost my way. Suddenly, I found that I simply did not know what to *do*. Concealing my barrenness and distress, I took myself that summer to a nearby convalescent home and offered my services as "a volunteer." I was secretly hoping that some old wise person, contemplating his own imminent death, would somehow give me a clue as to *what* I was supposed to do. Mainly, I played cards with people in desperate physical straits and saw suffering all around. And our conversations were mostly about how well someone had played a hand of bridge or when the refreshments would be brought in. Philosophical ruminations on life were not in vogue.

It was while I was vainly seeking "the answer" at the convalescent home that I happened to read Moody's book.

During the thirteen months of interviewing near-death survivors, I received my answer. The professor had found his teacher at last. They were ordinary people who described, in a consistent way, an extraordinary patterning of experiences which occurs at the point of death. The effect of personally seeing this pattern gradually reveal itself over the course of these interviews is something

I shall probably never adequately be able to convey. But this effect, combined with that quality of luminous serenity which many near-death survivors manifest, made me feel that I myself was undergoing an extended religious awakening.

Quite a few of my interviewees claimed or believed that during their experiences they encountered God directly or sensed His presence intuitively. It was really astonishing how often this was asserted by persons of all sorts of religious persuasions including non-believers. What to make of such statements is, of course, another matter. Professional interpreters can debate the question. As for me, I can only say that I have no doubt I saw Him, too. He left His mark on those I talked to. And they left their mark on me.

NDEs: The Early Years – A Personal History

I figure that before I kick the bucket, I should take the time to set down something of my personal story of how I became one of the early pioneers to study NDEs and, not long after, to co-found IANDS, the International Association for Near-Death Studies. After all, I am one of the few who was there at the beginning and would like to take you back to those exciting days of high adventure at the outset of my life in NDEland. So, gather round, friends, sit a spell and I will tell you the tale of the how it came to pass that I got involved with NDEs and how IANDS was born.

In the summer of 1976, I was mired in the waning and turbulent days of a disastrous marriage, which would soon implode in violence and mayhem, causing me untold anguish as I reeled from the centrifugal winds that blew my marriage and my life to bits. But, fortunately, that's not the personal history that's relevant here, though for drama and trauma, it certainly made that year a pivotal one in my life. But a few months earlier, something else happened that would prove to be even more monumental for me, a life-changing event from which I would never recover.

I remember the day it happened. It's still vivid in my mind. I was sitting outside my house at the time, a few miles down the road from the University of Connecticut. It was summer and the weather was sunny and pleasant. I was reading a book. Hardly anyone had heard of it. Its author was a psychiatrist whose name was unfamiliar to me: Raymond A. Moody, Jr. The book, of course, as you now will have realized, was *Life After Life.*

As I read it with mounting excitement, and started making furious marginal notes, I remember thinking, "This is it!" I knew immediately and intuitively that I would want to do my own research on what Moody had dubbed "near-death experiences." Moody was not a scientist (he had actually taught philosophy before turning to medicine), and his book was mainly a collection of anecdotes. But as an academic psychologist, I fancied myself a scientist, and before I had finished the book, the outlines of the research I would soon initiate were already clear in my mind. I was on fire, already thrilled at the prospect of learning more about what it was like to die and live to tell the tale.

It's funny how sometimes things just slide into place without one's lifting a finger, so to speak. Because what happened next, just within a day or three, is that several of my students – I had a small coterie of devoted students then – came by and in effect asked me what I was up to these days. "Funny you should ask," I might have said, but didn't. But when I told them what I had in mind, they picked up on my enthusiasm and asked if they could get involved. In short order, I had the makings of a research team, which would soon expand to more than a half dozen students, mostly undergraduates.

Meanwhile, I was already hard at work drafting a grant proposal. My plan was to see if I could work with a number of hospitals in the Hartford area and, with their consent, get referrals to patients who had come close to death. I was both surprised and delighted soon to learn that the University Research Foundation approved my proposal and had funded it fully. Surprised because, remember, at that time hardly anyone had heard of NDEs or if they had were not likely to give them any credence. Nevertheless, I was off and running – to Hartford.

In short order, I had made contact with the appropriate administrators and physicians at three hospitals in Hartford (as well as several other potential sources of respondents) and gave my first lecture at Hartford Hospital to discuss NDEs and my proposed research. Again I was surprised that the response I received was positive. People came up afterward to say they would be delighted to help me. Another door opening for me with my barely touching it. I am no great scholar, God knows, but I do have – or did have – charm in those days, and I think that helped to persuade the powers that be that I would not bring disgrace to their institutions.

Soon I was striding the halls of Hartford Hospital, wearing a while lab coat, as if I were a "real doctor," on my way to interview patients who were recovering from a serious near-death incident. Of course, I had no idea whether they had had an NDE. All I could know is that they had apparently been close to death. But with my third patient, I hit pay dirt. To this day, I remember her name – Iris Lemov – who had had a close call owing to a severe case of Crohn's Disease. Iris confided in me that she did experience something unusual when she was very ill and went on to describe a classic Moody-type NDE. I could hardly conceal my excitement. I was finding exactly what Moody had reported in his book, *Life After Life*.

Originally, I had thought I would train my students, especially my graduate students, to conduct most of these interviews, but after doing a few of them myself, I decided that I wanted to do as many as possible. In the end, I wound up interviewing about three-quarters of my sample of 102 persons who had come close to death.

Now, here's another door that opened for me when I all I had to do was to approach it. Years of subsequent research have shown that only a small percentage – usually around 15% – of persons who come close to death and survive report an NDE afterward. But in my study, which I described at length in my first NDE book, *Life at Death,* I found that almost half of my patients (or former patients) recounted an NDE. So I had gobs of data, and without going into detail here, what I found fully confirmed and extended Moody's original anecdotal findings. *Life at Death* is now regarded as the first rigorous scientific study of NDEs.

Most of the people I eventually interviewed were no longer hospitalized, however. Instead, I would bomb around the state of Connecticut in my trusty Dodge Dart to conduct my interviews and then play the tape on the way home. I can't begin to describe the profound emotions I felt doing these interviews as people recounted, often with tears, what they had experienced when close to death. Often, I was the first person to hear their story. There was usually a feeling of a sacred encounter taking place between us as people shared with me what they claimed to be the most important thing that had ever happened to them. I felt both privileged and blessed to be entrusted with their most treasured, if sometimes perplexing, near-death episode.

After spending thirteen months tracking down and interviewing my respondents, one day I was sitting outside on the deck of the house where I was then living, working at a picnic table, tabulating and analyzing my data. And with paper and pencil, if you can believe it. Remember, this was in the late 1970s at a time before computers were common, and when there was no Internet and when no one had ever heard of a cell phone. We were still in the typewriter age then.

But I remember that day because my then girlfriend Norma came over, and I still recall what I said to her when I looked up from my data sheets. "No one is going to believe this, Norma. I am sitting on dynamite!" I already knew that I had struck a vein of gold.

Not long afterward, one evening in 1977 I was in my kitchen, stirring some cream sauce, when the phone rang. Still stirring the pot, I reached across for the phone and heard an unfamiliar voice on the line speaking with a southern accent.

"Hello, Ken? This is Raymond Moody."

"No shit?" I replied.

I stopped stirring my cream sauce.

Raymond wanted to invite me to Charlottesville, Virginia, where he then lived. Several researchers of whom he had heard were following up on his work, and someone had drawn his attention to me. That someone – a sociologist colleague of Moody's named John Audette – would soon be in touch about the arrangements, but meanwhile Raymond was hoping I could come down.

Could I!

On November 19, 1977, one of my research associates, Sue Palmer, who had been of inestimable help to me in carrying out my original research, and I loaded up my car and headed down to Virginia where I would meet not only Raymond, but several other professionals who would come to play key pioneering roles in the development of the field of near-death studies – in particular, Bruce Greyson, Michael Sabom and John Audette, all of whom were to become close colleagues of mine. Everything of importance really began from that first meeting. And one of the most significant decisions to come out of that meeting was the intention to form some kind of professional association to promote the scientific study of NDEs.

Some months later, in August, 1978, Greyson, Sabom, Audette and I met at a conference where we established an organization to further the professional study of NDEs, which Audette headed for a couple of years. We gave it a stuffy, high-flalutin academic name: The Association for the Scientific Study of Near-Death Phenomena. The reason for doing this was to try to interest other professionals and academics in the study of NDEs.

Here's what we looked like at that time. The bespectacled guy in a suit on the left is me; above me is John Audette. Next to him is Bruce Greyson and then Mike Sabom. We had a dream....

Meanwhile, I was working furiously to complete my book, *Life At Death.* I was lucky enough to find an agent for it and before I knew it, I learned that there was actually a bidding war going on for my book. I was amazed because I was at the time a completely unknown author – just a professor of no particular distinction and no professional reputation at all. Nevertheless, my book seemed to be a hot commodity and I finally accepted an offer from a then well knowns publisher. My editor soon became the head of the publishing firm, and I was thrilled to have her to advise me. I still remember how she courted me. She took me to "her table" at the fabled Four Seasons restaurant. I remember only one thing that happened at the outset of our lunch that day. She reached across the table, and solemnly placing her hand on mine, told me, "This is just the beginning, Ken."

Wow, who me? But in a way, she was right. She quickly set up an extensive book tour for me, and in those days there were many television shows where authors like me would be invited to hawk their books. In short order, I was a guest on all the popular network shows of that era – Good Morning America, The Today Show, Donahue, Larry King, and so many more – dozens, probably, and radio shows, too. I was interviewed by then famous anchors, such as Tom Brokaw, and met other celebrities who were also guests on those shows. My biggest thrill was meeting some baseball heroes of my youth – Yankee pitcher, Whitey Ford, and Los Angeles catcher, Roy Campanella. I also recall being with Carol Channing ("Hello, Dolly!") in the green room of one program where she looked – no disrespect – like a old hag. Until she went on when she was transformed into the dynamic stage star she had long been famous for. It *was* a heady time for me. My fifteen minutes of minor celebrity. I tried not to let it go to my head, which fortunately remained attached to my neck. That wasn't too hard because my book never became a best seller, though it did respectably. But after that, I was often "in demand" and had more offers for speaking engagements than I could accommodate.

Now back to earth.

Late in 1980, after my whirlwind book tour was over, John Audette asked me if I would take it over the organization he had been heading and run it "for a year" while he devoted himself to NDE research. I agreed, but with conditions. I wanted to re-name it and call it The International Association for Near-Death Studies (IANDS) and make it into a dues-paying membership organization. I also would establish a headquarters for it at The University of Connecticut, where I then taught, and found a scholarly NDE journal, etc. All of which I was able to do, thanks to the invaluable support of Greyson and Audette -- and a lot of help from my friends and probably a few angels as well. Anyway, after my meeting with Audette, I went to work.

I first approached my department head at the university and managed to get an old unused office (we eventually needed three) to set up shop, and then I recruited a bunch of my students to help run it. A then-graduate student (who eventually became an English professor and poet) named Steve Straight was one of my main assistants, and he edited the newsletter, which I had named *Vital Signs*. In those days before desktop publishing, everything had to be done by hand. We would stay up all night doing paste-up to get the newsletter out on time. Then several volunteers and I would crowd into the office, affix labels, munch pizza, and cart the things over to the Post Office and send them out. A student of mine, Leah Andrews, with her faithful dog Pardner, ran the office then and helped me with the mountains of correspondence that soon started flooding in. A dreamy art student named Ned Kahn (who later became a world-famous environmental artist and MacArthur grant recipient) designed the original IANDS logo.

We had fun, we had a wonderful *esprit de corps*, though some weeks I worked a hundred hours between running IANDS, teaching at the university, editing our journal, and shooting my mouth off at lectures around the country. I was young then. We had a ball, and we didn't spend a cent on salaries. That was what IANDS was like in the early days. Nothing would have been possible, though, without the tireless and devoted help of those students. And those angels who must have guided our efforts.

But my NDE life was not confined to the university. No, it had already spilled over to my home, which I now shared with my then love, Norma, and our children (from our previous marriages). At that time, we lived in a beautiful old house on the banks of the Mt. Hope River. The house had a storied history from colonial times (guess who was rumored to have slept there?) and had once been a converted inn. We came to call it "The Near-Death Hotel," and sometimes, as a joke, hoisted up a banner on the porch between the house's stately pillars with that name proclaimed for all the neighbors and passersby to gawk at.

My home soon became a kind of informal center for near-death studies. Steve Straight lived there for a couple of years as did a nurse from Spain, Maria Castedo, who was passionate about NDEs. (I have remained in touch with them both.) As for Norma, who was really the heart of the near-death hotel, we lived as man and wife though we never married. (After three failed marriages, I had promised my daughter, Kathryn, I would never marry again.) But since everything was near-this and near-that, Norma became my "near-wife."

Once my book had come out, NDErs from all over sought me out and quite a few eventually arrived and stayed with us in what we came to call "the near-death room." Some of these persons were memorable characters. There was Patrick Gallagher, who had once been a distinguished university professor of anthropology, but after his NDE, he became a kind of Whitmanesque character bumming around the country. He lived in California, but he was so taken with my book, he decided to hitchhike to Connecticut so he could tell me about his NDE, which took place (I am not making this up) in Death Valley. He stayed with us for a month and entertained us and my other guests greatly with his yarns. Then there was Tom Sawyer (yes, his actual name), one of the most remarkable NDErs I ever met. I wrote about Tom in my next book, *Heading Toward Omega,* but he deserves a book of his own, and in fact two have been written about him. Professionals interested in NDEs came, too, such as Margot Grey from England, who eventually published an important book on NDEs. And then there was Blaine Bostock, a kind of refugee from a Swedenborgian community in Pennsylvania, which I had visited since Swedenborgians were keen on NDEs. But Blaine deserves a special introduction.

You see, one morning I woke up with a near-death ditty on my mind. I remember that day, too, because the lyrics for the song came, like Athena from Zeus's head, virtually fully formed without my having to do more than write them down. Sung to the tune of Gene Autry's theme song, "Back in the Saddle," it went like this:

I'm out of my body at last
Seein' my future and my past
Floating through tunnel now,
I look around say, "oh wow!"
It's so peaceful here,
I don't feel no kind of fear."
Just driftin' and singin' my song
Oh Lord, why's this tunnel so long?

But what's that ahead of me?
Is that a golden light I see?
The face of God shines through
And I'm headin' straight for you

(In a basso profundo, as befits God)

My son, you have much work to do
And your family and friends need you, too
So I'm sending you back
One more chance to get on track
You'll come to me later
(Ritardando) On my cosmic elevator

(In a natural but awed voice)

I'm back in my body again,
Wonderin' what happened just then
Was that the Lord above
Did I just imagine all that love?
I reckon I'll know one day for sure
(Ritardando) I reckon I'll know one day for sure

[Da-dum (dominant-tonic) on the guitar....]

Sometimes when we would have an IANDS board meeting at my home, I would be asked to sing that song before we got to work. It always got a laugh and put us in a good mood. But I also took it on the road. Once I sang it close up to Elizabeth Kubler-Ross at her farm in Virginia. Another time, at the Omega Institute in New York, where I was doing a workshop, I had the chance to sing it to Pete Seeger, who looked completely baffled (he had no idea what I was singing about) as well as to Bobby McFerrin, who seemed amused. Somebody eventually told me that someone had brought the song to the attention of Willie Nelson who said he wanted to record it, but of course he never did.

I had no shame singing it on occasion at some of the conferences I attended at the conclusion of my lecture. I remember once, in Prague, in front of an audience of 2000, I sang it and got one of the few standing O's I've ever received. I don't know how my talk was received, but my song was a hit!

Which brings us back to Blaine, who was a musician and gui-
tarist. Naturally, I sang it for Blaine, and it inspired him to write his
own near-death songs, which he would then sing at local clubs. I
remember he had one called "The Near-Death Hotel," and another,
"Tiptoe through the Tunnel." Blaine stayed with us for a month,
too.

Raymond Moody never had much interest in IANDS as such,
but of course we all were very fond of Raymond, who was a
delight and has a marvelous sense of humor. He would often crack
us up with his wit. Sometimes we'd all troop down to his farm in
Virginia to hold our board meetings there. Here's a photograph of
"the four amigos" with Raymond who loved to sit in his rocking
chair during these affairs:

In those early days of IANDS, when I was serving as its President and genial dictator, I was also doing my best to raise funds for
the organization since, I must confess, most of our board members
didn't do squat in that regard. I never liked having to make a pitch
for IANDS with potential wealthy benefactors, but it did give me the

opportunity to spend time with the moneyed crowd in Palm Beach, with politicians like the longtime senator from Rhode Island, Claiborne Pell, and with his pal, one of the princes of Lichtenstein. And then there was a wealthy man of mystical leanings in Malibu where he lived in a palatial house once owned by the Aga Khan who had been married to the actress, Rita Hayworth. When I stayed there, I slept in a vast bedroom called "The Rita Hayworth" room. This man had a large following of Hollywood types and minor celebrities, like "Miss Oil of Olay," next to whom I sat at one lavish dinner, and a runner-up in a Miss America contest. It turned out this man was a leader of some kind of cult, but when I declined to be initiated, he booted me out.

Well, those were the days, my friends, but they had to end, at least for me. After serving two terms as President of IANDS, I was due for a sabbatical and asked Bruce Greyson to relieve me of the responsibility of editing our NDE journal. He not only consented, but edited it for the next twenty-five years and turned it into a first-rate scholarly journal. Meanwhile I returned to my research, writing, lecturing and my day job as a professor at UCONN.

Here's a photo of Bruce and me from those days, which was taken at one of those board meetings. Brothers, we were:

IANDS subsequently went through various existential and financial crises, and moved around a lot, but now more than forty years later, it is going strong and is more successful than ever. It still publishes *The Journal of Near-Death Studies* and its quarterly newsletter, now in digital form. And of course there are now probably more than a thousand articles in the professional literature on NDEs and scads of books, YouTube videos of NDErs, etc. We had a dream – and it came true.

As for me, I'm back in the saddle again, just riding a different horse until I get to that last round-up in the sky.

Contemplating One's Own Death

Waiting to Die

The bright realization that must come before death will be worth all the boredom of living.

— Ned Rorem

What's it like, waiting to die? Of course, it's different for everyone. I can only say what it's like for me. On the whole, it's rather boring.

Don't get me wrong. I still have many pleasures in life and – knock on silicon – I'm lucky not to be suffering from any fatal illness, though if I were, that would certainly add some drama in my life. I could then follow the example of the poet Ted Rosenthal, who after contracting leukemia, joyfully called his friends and said, "Guess what's happened to *me!*" Well, no thanks. I'll take my boring life any day and intone a hymn of gratitude every morning I wake up with only the ordinary indignities of an old man – coughing, wheezing and sneezing, and, oh, my aching back!

But still … I'm used to having productive work – writing books, helping other authors with their books, being involved in various professional pursuits, and so forth. But recently I published my last book, which I puckishly entitled, *Pieces of My Mind Before I Fall to Pieces,* which was a kind of potpourri of stories and interests from my later years, and just after that I wrote what I expect to be my last professional article, the foreword to a colleague's memoir. Now what? More precisely, what do I do with my time now that I have clearly entered the epilogue to my life? Honestly, I feel as if I have stepped over the threshold into my afterlife before dying.

Of course, I can watch films – I've become quite a "film buff" in my later years; I still have interesting books to read. I am blessed with a wonderful girlfriend. Still, since life has become a spectator sport for me, and I can no longer travel, except locally, I find that I am spending more time on my sofa, honing my couch potato skills, watching sports. Yet I must confess that even they have lost a good deal of their zest for me. My home town baseball team, The San Francisco Giants, finished in the cellar last year; in golf, Tiger has gone away; in basketball, Michael Jordan is long gone; and in tennis, which is now the only sport I follow with some avidity, it is chiefly because of the great Roger Federer. Nevertheless, I can only wonder how long he can at 36 continue to produce one miracle after another? Surely, he, too, will begin his inevitable decline soon, and with his descent from the heights of glory, my interest in tennis will also flag. So what will be left then? I will tell you.

The body. Mine. It has already become my principal preoccupation and *bête-noire*. These days, I can't help recalling that St. Francis referred to the body as "brother ass." It seems I now spend most of my time in doctors', chiropractors' or dentists' clinics, as they strive to preserve my decaying body parts by inflicting various forms of torture on me that would even impress Torquemada, or doing physical therapy in what is most likely a vain attempt to delay the encroaching onset of wholesale physical deterioration. Really, is this any way to run a navy? There are many days when I think the only surgery that will preserve me would be a complete bodyectomy.

Well, okay, I realize this is only par for the course of the everyday life of an octogenarian. Wasn't it Bette Davis who famously said "old age is no place for sissies?" It isn't for wimps like me either, it seems. (I can often be heard crooning, "turn back the hands of time….") Still, I wouldn't go so far as the saturnine Philip Roth who said that old age is "a massacre." I guess at this point I find myself somewhere between Davis and Roth, but the waiting game still seems to be a losing proposition and I might very well come to think of my current boredom as the halcyon days of my decline.

Nevertheless, consider a typical day in the life of this old wheezing geezer.

It begins with the back. Every day does. In the morning, you get up, but your back doesn't. It hurts. Even though you take a hot shower before bed, by the time you wake up your back has decided to take the day off. When you try to use it, as for example, when you bend over to pick up the comb you've dropped into the toilet, it begins to complain. And finally, it gets so bad, you have to lie down on your once neatly made bed, remove half your clothing, and apply some ice to it while listening to mindless music and cursing the day when some enterprising hominid decided it would be a good idea to change from the arboreal life to a bipedal one. Big mistake. The next one was the invention of agriculture, but never mind. We were talking about the back and its vicissitudes.

Nevertheless, a little later, you decide to take your body out of a spin. "Don't look back," the great Satchel Paige advised, "something might be gaining on you." In my case, it's the man with the scythe whom I hope to outstrip for a few more years.

Of course, the back, which had only been moaning quietly before now begins to object vociferously, asking sourly, "what the hell are you thinking?" Nevertheless, you press on, thinking your will will prevail, and your back can go to hell.

But the next dispiriting thing you notice are all these chubby old ladies whizzing by you as if they are already late for their hair appointments. How humiliating – to be passed by these old biddies! You think about the days in junior high when you were a track star, setting school records in the dashes and anchoring the relay races, which you used to run in your bare feet. Then you ran like the wind. These days, you are merely winded after trudging a hundred yards.

When you can go no further, you turn around only to become aware of still another distressing sight. Actually, it *is* your sight

– or lack of it. It ain't working. You could see pretty well after your corneal surgery last year, but now you can't see worth shit. What is that ahead of you? Is it a woolly mammoth, a Saint Bernard or merely a burly ex-football player? Where are the eyes of yester-year? Gone missing. Well, they didn't give me any guarantees as to how long my vision would last before it decided, like my back, to begin to object to its continued use outdoors. The way of all flesh doesn't stop with the flesh; it continues with the cornea, so now I am cursing the darkness in the middle of a miasmal morning.

I finally arrive home in a disconsolate mood, but now it is time to hop onto my stationary bike, which is the only kind I have ever been able to ride since my balance is worse than that of an elderly inebriate on New Year's Eve. I used to be able to pedal reasonably fast and for a long time. But lately someone must have snuck in to affix some kind of a brake to the bike since suddenly it seems that I am pumping uphill at an acute angle. Heart rate is up, speed is down, my old distance marks are a treasured memory, which I can only mourn. All I am aware of now is the sound of someone huffing and puffing.

At last the torture is over, but now I really have to piss. That damn enlarged prostate of mine has no patience – it must be sat-isfied *now!* I race into the bathroom, unzip my fly before it is too late, and make sure, because I have my girlfriend's admonitions in my ears as I piss that she will behead me if I continue to treat the floor as an auxiliary pissoir, I am pissing very carefully into the toilet bowl. Of course, these days, my urinary stream is a some-times thing. It starts, it stops, it pauses to refresh itself, it pulses, stops, dribbles, starts up again with what seems to be its last mighty effort to produce something worthwhile and finally drips itself into extinction.

I'm relieved, however, because at least I haven't soiled my pants this time. But wait. What is that? Pulling up my pants, I can feel some urine on my left thigh. How the hell did it get in there? Is there some kind of silent secondary stream that runs down the side of my leg when I am otherwise preoccupied with trying to keep my penile aim from going astray?

Now I have to find a towel to wipe off the offending liquid and just hope my girlfriend won't say, when I return to the kitchen, "what is that funny smell, darling?"

Well, you get the idea. Life is no longer a bowl of cherries, or if it is, some of them are turning rotten. And naturally I can't help wondering how long I have to go before I *really* cross that final threshold over the unknown. For years, I've joked that I've wanted to live to be 1000 – months – old. Now I'm at 984 and counting. I'm getting close, and it's no longer just a joke.

And of course I now also have to wonder what will be next? I mean, after I die, assuming I will ever get around to it.

Well, in my case, I have some inklings because I've spent half my life researching and writing about near-death experiences and in the course of my work I've interviewed hundreds of people who have told me what it was like for them to die – at least for a few moments – before returning to life. And what they have told me has been, I am frank to admit, profoundly reassuring.

I remember one woman who said that in order to grasp the feeling of peace that comes with death you would have to take the thousand best things that ever happened to you, multiply them by a million and *maybe,* she said (I remember her emphasis on the word, "maybe"), you could come close to that feeling. Another man said that if you were to describe the feelings of peace that accompanied death, you would have to write it in letters a mile high. All this might sound hyperbolic, but I have heard such sentiments from many near-death experiencers. Here's just one more specific quote from a man I knew very well for many years, telling me what it was like for him to die:

> It was a total immersion in light, brightness, warmth, peace, security ... I just immediately went into this beautiful bright light. It's difficult to describe .... Verbally, it cannot be expressed. It's something which becomes you

and you become it. I could say "I was peace, I was love."
I was the brightness. It was part of me …. You just know.
You're all-knowing – and everything is a part of you. It's
just so beautiful. It was eternity. It's like I was always there
and I will always be there, and my existence on earth was
just a brief instant.

After listening to so many people describe what it was like
for them to die, it is easy for me to imagine what it might be like
for me – for anyone – to take that final journey. And many great
writers have said much the same thing as those I have interviewed
have told me about what is in store when we die. Walt Whitman,
for example, who wrote "And I will show that nothing can happen
more beautiful than death." And Herman Melville, with even more
eloquence, said, "And death, which alike levels all, alike impresses
all with a last revelation, which only an author from the death could
adequately tell." It seems that in our own time, these authors from
the death are today's near-death experiencers, and the revelations
they have shared with us appear fully to support the claims of these
famous 19th century American authors.

So having immersed myself in the study of near-death experiences for so many years, I'm actually looking forward to my
passage when my time comes. Still, I'm not looking forward to
the dying part. In that regard, I'm with Woody Allen who quipped,
"I'm not afraid of death; I just don't want to be there when it
happens." I just hope that all those stories I've heard about how
wonderful death itself is aren't some kind of a spiritual *trompe
l'oeil,* a cosmic joke played by a malevolent god. Or as that mar-
velously antic diarist and composer, Ned Rorem, whimsically
jested, "If, after dying, I discover there is no Life After Death, will
I be furious?"

Of course, when I am faced with the imminence of death, I
hope I'll be able to comport myself with some equanimity, but
who knows? Think of Seneca who wrote so eloquently about
suicide, and then horribly botched his own. Well, naturally, I'm not

planning to hasten my death by such extravagant means, though I wouldn't refuse a kind offer of a little help from my doctor friends to ease me on my way if I'm having trouble giving birth to my death. It can, after all, be a labor-intensive enterprise. I just hope I can find myself on that stairway to heaven I've heard so much about and can manage to avoid a trip in the opposite direction.

Meanwhile, when did you say Federer will be playing his next match?

The Body Is a Sometimes Thing

The blind receive sight and the lame walk, the lepers are cleansed and the deaf hear, and the dead are raised up.
– Matthew, 11:5

Death is no more than passing from one room into another. But there's a difference for me, you know. Because in that other room I shall be able to see.
– Helen Keller

A middle-aged man, with a paunch, is sitting on a doctor's examining table waiting anxiously for the doctor to return with the results of his latest examination.

The doctor comes in, looking solemn.

"I'm afraid it's your body," he intones.

I am that man. Surely Yeats did not have me or my body in mind when he wrote his immortal lines, "things fall apart, the center cannot hold," but they are apposite, I'm afraid. Somatic entropy is icumen in.

I don't want to bore you with a list of my various infirmities and debilities since I already regaled you with those woes in the very first essay in this series, which I wrote in December, 2017. I'm tempted just to write something along the lines of, "suffice it to say, they have all grown worse." But I will resist that temptation if you will indulge me for a few moments in order to give you some specifics. Besides, as usual, I have an ulterior motive for mentioning some of them, which will shortly be revealed.

To begin with, I now list. That is, these days when standing or walking, I am no longer an orthogonal being. Instead, following my political proclivities, I tilt to the left. Generally, I am not aware of this until I run into a lamppost or something, which is a painful way of being reminded that I now am an embodiment of the same principle as the Leaning Tower of Pisa.

And then there is my difficulty in walking, quite apart from my wayward posture. For one thing, I have now acquired not just a paunch of my own, but a pot. I joke that having once written a book entitled *Heading Toward Omega,* I could now write another called *Heading Toward Rotundity.* Hell, I am only heading toward death, but I have already achieved full rotundity. And this in a man who was once described as a "slender mustachioed researcher." The pounds don't come off easily any longer; they adhere, having found a cozy home of their own in my belly and seek to expand like a balloon filling with air, even when I *think* about consuming another York Mint Patty. The result is, I no longer just walk; it's more that I now waddle, and sometimes wobble, in the general direction of my destination, drawing piteous and condescending stares, and sometimes curses, from the buff young Marinites who have to swerve to avoid hitting me with their bikes on the walking path that runs along the creek adjacent to my home.

But that's only the beginning of my current travails. Worse still is what causes me to mutter, "ai, ai, eye!" Yes, it's my eye, or rather it's the lack of vision in one of them. (And, BTW, I can't resist mentioning to you that for years I saw an eye doctor named – Dr. Ai. No, I am not kidding. He was a retinal specialist, and that was really his name. I managed to refrain making the obvious joke whenever I saw him.) But back to my eyes.

I have had glaucoma for over twenty years, and recently it's got quite a bit worse. When you have glaucoma you are regularly tested to see how much peripheral vision you have lost. Would you like to see the latest results for my right eye? Please take a look at the diagram below.

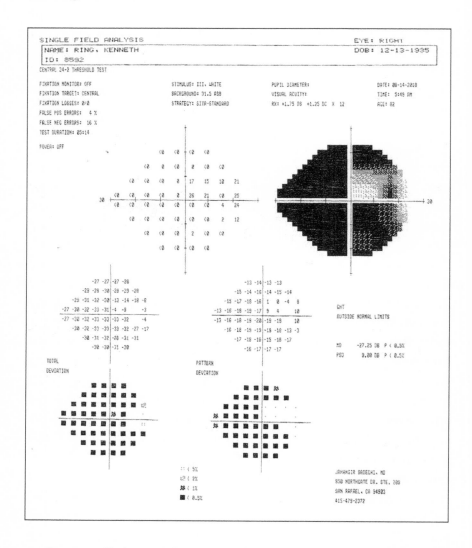

Ignore all the numbers. Just look at the picture with all the black shading. Wherever you see black, that's what I *don't* see. So, you can see that I am completely blind on the left side of that eye, and have only a little sliver of vision in my right visual field. In addition, I have what's called a macular pucker (or wrinkle) in that eye that interferes with my central vision. When I try to look at the Snellen chart (the chart that eye doctors use to check your vision), the best I can do is 20/200.

So to put all this into technical terms, that eye is shot. In order to see anything, I have to depend on my left eye, which isn't nearly so compromised by glaucoma, but it ain't so great either.

Are you beginning to get an idea of my visual world? Unfortunately, my vision has deteriorated quite a bit since I started writing these essays. Nowadays, I don't see as much as I *infer* the existence of what we were once pleased to call the external world. I mean, if the street where I walk was there yesterday, I assume it must still be there today. But my vision is getting to be a joke. For example, the other day, as I was completing my warm-down after my stint on my stationary bike, I happened to pass by my next door neighbor, who was walking her dog. I did recognize that a dog was coming toward me, but I failed to recognize my neighbor. Just call me Mr. Magoo of Marin.

Well, you can see – no pun intended since that verb is largely conjectural for me now – that I have my reasons for hoping that I won't have to wait too much longer to have better vision. No, there is no operation that can help me.

The only thing that can – is death! And now I will tell you why I have cause to think that one day, perhaps before too long, I will have *perfect* vision.

One of things that first struck me so forcibly when I was starting out on my life as an NDE researcher was how often my respondents would comment on how well they could see (and hear) during their NDEs. Here are some of those remarks from my first book on NDEs, *Life at Death.*

I could see very clearly, yeh, yeh. I recognized it [her body] as being me.

My ears were very sensitive at that point... Vision also.

I heard everything clearly and distinctly.

Seems like everything was clear. My hearing was clear ... I felt like I could hear a pin drop. My sight – everything was clear.

It was as if my whole body had eyes and ears.

Years later, one of my students, who had had an NDE, and who had previously lost most of the hearing in one of his ears, told me he could hear *perfectly* during his NDE.

And it's a similar story for people who are poorly sighted, but not during their NDE. Consider the following case of a 48-year-old woman who reported this experience following post-surgical complications. All of a sudden:

Bang. I left. The next thing I was aware of was floating on the ceiling. And seeing down there, with his hat on his head [she is referring to her anesthesiologist] *... it was so vivid. I'm very near-sighted, too, by the way, which was another one of the startling things that happened when I left my body. I see at fifteen feet what most people see at 400 ... They were hooking me up to a machine behind my head. And my first thought was, "Jesus, I can see! I can't believe it, I can see!" I could read the numbers on the machine behind my head and I was just so thrilled. And I thought, "They gave me back my glasses."*

Things were enormously clear and bright ... From where I was looking, I could look down on this enormous fluorescent light... and it was so dirty on top of the light. [Could you see the top of the light fixture, then? I asked.] *I was floating above the light fixture.* [Could you see the top of the light fixture?] *Yes* [sounding a little impatient with my question], *and it was filthy. And I remember thinking, "Got to tell the nurses about that."*

Even more astonishing than the fact that those with defective vision seem to see perfectly during their NDE is the finding from my own research on the blind (he said modestly) that clearly shows that even persons who are congenitally blind – people who obviously have never seen in their lives – *can* and do see during their NDEs. As one of these persons who I interviewed for my book, *Mindsight,* where I present about thirty of these cases, and who had had two NDEs, said: "Those experiences were the only time I could ever relate to seeing, and to what light was, because I experienced it. I was able to see."

This testimony comes from a woman named Vicki who was 43 when I first met and interviewed her in Seattle. In the course of her interview she told me that during her (second) NDE, when she was 22, which took place in a hospital, she found herself up by the ceiling and could clearly see her body below (she recognized it from seeing her hair and also her wedding ring). She continued to ascend and eventually came to be *above* the hospital, where she saw streets, buildings and the lights of the city. She also told me that she saw different intensities of brightness and wondered if that was what people meant when they referred to colors.

Vicki was only one such case of the congenitally blind who reported some kind of vision during their NDE; as I've mentioned, there were others. How such eyeless vision, which I called mindsight, can occur is something I speculate about in my book, but the fact that it occurs is incontestable, however inexplicable it appears.

What does all this research have to tell us about the kind of body we may find ourselves in after death? Of course, no one can say with certainty, but the implication is that it will be one in which all of the senses we have in our earthly body are somehow able to function with perfect clarity. And if that's so, it stands to reason that whatever infirmities or physical limitations we have here will be absent *there.*

Think of it this way. When we dream, we are usually not aware of any bodily limitations. Indeed, we may not even be aware of having a "dream body." I know that in my own dreams, I am aware of myself, but not my body. Now, don't misunderstand: An NDE is in no way like a dream; it is far more real. From the standpoint of an NDE, it is *more* real than what we call life, and certainly more real than even the most vivid dream. Nevertheless, our dreams are perhaps the best intimation of the wonders that await us after we die. And in that state, the one that we can anticipate when we die, all bodily malfunctions appear to be transcended.

When I contemplate such possibilities, I know it makes it a lot easier for me to deal with the signs of my own creeping decrepitude and my increasingly poor vision. I know that they are only the temporary impediments of my aging body.

In any case, you can now understand that I am not just waiting to die. I'm waiting to *see.* Perfectly.

Is Death the End or the Beginning?

The Great Debate:
Is Death a Dead End?

Of course, when you're in that in-between zone – what the Tibetans call a "bardo" – after your life is over but before you've died, you have plenty of time to think – to ruminate and to wonder what will happen to you when you finally cross that threshold and enter the house of death.

Oh, perhaps before I follow that train of thought, I guess I should clarify what I meant when I wrote that line about my life being over. Obviously, either I'm still here or a ghost is writing this. What I meant was that the really active part of my life has finished – no more love affairs, exciting adventures, extensive travels, doing research, writing books, and so forth – all the activities that I enjoyed so much during my life until recent years. Yes, I still have my quieter pleasures, as I have written, but mostly I am just waiting – waiting to die. And can't help speculating what will happen once I do.

Lately, I have been reading a little philosophy, not about life and death matters, but in doing so, it has occurred to me that so many of the world's great thinkers are professed atheists and are convinced that when we die, that's it. Poof! Death brings annihilation to our individual personalities and to all consciousness. We enter into a sleep from which we never awaken.

Let's consider this roster of the world's greatest minds who hold this view. There's Friedrich Nietzsche, of course, who became the most influential philosopher of the 19th century, albeit only after he had gone mad in 1889 while embracing a horse that was being beaten on the streets of Turin. And then there was Heidegger, commonly regarded as the greatest philosopher of the 20th century despite his unapologetic embrace of and involvement with Nazism. But let's not get distracted.

Another unabashed atheist who immediately comes to mind (at least mine) of whom you have doubtless heard is a fellow named Sigmund Freud, unquestionably one of the most influential thinkers of the 20th century. And then I immediately think of the psychoanalytically-inclined anthropologist, Ernest Becker, whose Pulitzer prize-winning book, *The Denial of Death,* I used to assign in one of my classes. Becker, incidentally, died before reaching the age of 50 and prepared for death by reading Chekhov, which I used to read to my mother before *she* died, but never mind. I seem to be digressing again, which may be my own way of denying death. Finally, we shouldn't overlook one of the most widely quoted philosophers of our own time, Woody Allen, who can be seen toting around Becker's book in his glorious smash hit, Annie Hall. And in another one of his top-rated films, Hannah and Her Sisters, his mordant character makes us laugh by reminding us that the universe is totally meaningless, which, leads him to consider becoming a Hare Krishna. Whatever works.

But let's continue our list of the world's most influential avowed atheists. No such list would be complete without mentioning the most revered and beloved scientist of our own time, the recently deceased Stephen Hawking whose incontestable genius was often compared to Einstein's. And how about another intellectual luminary, Steven Weinberg, one of the leading theoretical physicists of the present day and a Nobel Laureate to boot?

Then of course we have that clutch of infamous atheists – a quartet that includes Richard Dawkins, Daniel Dennett, Christopher Hitchens and Sam Harris – no intellectual slouches, these guys.

Well, when you consider the collective brain power and

enormous influence of these men – and of course they are all men (make of that what you will) -- the idea that death is not a dead end seems patently ludicrous, a childish fantasy for people who can't deal with the obvious fact that death brings only extinction. We like to imagine what most religions teach – that we will continue to exist even after death, but in light of all reason, this is pure balderdash.

Still, as we know, most people don't believe this is balderdash. Surveys consistently show that the vast majority of people, certainly in the United States, believe in some form of life after death. Also arrayed against the view of the intellectual giants I've mentioned is the testimony of literally thousands of near-death experiencers who have at least entered into the first stages of death, which so far as I know, none of the formidable thinkers cited above ever did before their deaths; that is, none of them is known to have had an NDE. I can only wonder if they had, whether they would have remained so sure of their position. In my research on NDEs, I can say that I have encountered more than a few former atheists who changed their mind after having had an NDE.

However that may be, almost all near-death experiencers become undeniably convinced that some form of postmortem existence awaits us all. Let me take just a few moments to offer some illustrative examples from those persons who have come the closest to crossing the bourne from which Shakespeare taught – wrongly, as it turns out – no traveler returns.

> *I was standing in a mist and I knew immediately that I had died. And I was so happy that I had died but I was still alive. And I can't tell you how I felt. It was, "Oh, God, I'm dead, but I'm here. I'm me. And I started pouring out these enormous feelings of gratitude because I still existed and yet I knew perfectly well that I had died.*
>
> *I know there is life after death. Nobody can shake my belief. I have no doubt – it's peaceful and nothing to be feared. I don't know what's beyond what I experienced, but*

it's plenty for me. I only know that death is not to be feared, only dying.

Upon entering that Light ... the atmosphere, the energy, it's total pure energy, it's total knowledge, it's total love – everything about it is definitely the afterlife if you will ... As a result of that [experience] I have little apprehension about dying my natural death ... because if death is anything like what I experienced, it's gotta be the most wonderful thing to look forward to, absolutely the most wonderful thing.

It gave me an answer to what I think everyone must wonder about at one time or another in this life. Yes, there is an afterlife! More beautiful than anything you can begin to imagine. Once you know it, there is nothing that can equal it. You just know!

What is striking about these quotes – and the literature on NDEs is replete with them – is not merely their unanimity of opinion, but the tone of absolute certitude that pervades them. Those who have left their bodies behind, even for a moment, know without a scintilla of doubt that they will continue to exist, as themselves, in another world of indescribable radiant beauty.

So where does that leave us? We have two diametrically opposed points of view to consider – that of the renowned and world-famous intellectual atheists I've cited and that of the thousands of unknown ordinary persons who have had NDEs. Take yer choice.

For atheists, however, the road stops here, and there is nothing further to add. But the testimony of NDEs tells us that there is something more that awaits us after death, even if they can't tell us what. The question is, is there a way to know, and, secondly, does it make sense to try to conceive of it while we are, like me, waiting to die?

The distinguished psychiatrist Carl Jung, who himself had a profound NDE when he was nearly seventy years old, was an ardent proponent of precisely this kind of imaginative exercise. In his captivating memoir, *Memories, Dreams, Reflections,* written toward the end of his life, he exhorts his readers as follows: "A man should be able to say he has done his best to form a conception of life after death, or to create some image of it – even if he must confess his failure. Not to have done so is a vital loss."

At the risk of disagreeing with the great man, I demur. In fact, I think it is a friggin' waste of time. I give several reasons for taking this position in my book, *Lessons from the Light,* but the one I would emphasize here is two-fold. First, of all, it is impossible to know what, if anything, is going to happen to us, and second, near-death experiencers themselves tend to shy away from these speculations, often implying that the world beyond death completely defies representation in ordinary language. After all, if such a task could daunt even a sublime poet like Dante, what could we expect from mere mortals when they try to describe their encounter with the ineffable?

But there is a third reason as well. Thinking about the afterlife, assuming it exists, which honesty compels us to admit we can't know for certain in any case, keeps us from paying attention to our lives here, which is the *only* thing we *can* be certain of. Didn't Ram Dass remind us, in the title of his seminal book of wisdom, *Be Here Now*?

When the time comes for us to die, either we'll find out or we won't. Why waste time thinking about it now? I'm with Omar Khayyam on this one. The hell with it. I'm going to the movies with my girlfriend. Afterward, we'll have our bread, cheese and wine, though probably in our case we'll substitute some chocolate confection for the wine. I'm alive now and, while I'm waiting to die, by jingo, I'm going to enjoy myself as long as I can.

What Hath Roth Wrought?

Philip Roth, who wrote so fiercely about the torments of aging and the calamity of approaching death, has died. In the end it was congestive heart failure that brought his long life to its close. His wait is over.

I can only wonder what his last days were like. I'd like to think they weren't what he had so long imagined them to be, and that he went easy into death with a sense of relief if not of hope. For as he often said, he had none where death was concerned. For him, death simply was extinction. The flickering flame of the candle of life would be snuffed out for good and after that – no after, no nothing, no more Phillip Roth.

In any event, when I heard the news about Roth's death at the age of 85, it was natural for me, as it was for millions of his readers, to think about the man – about his life and work, and perhaps his legacy. What had Roth wrought?

I was never a big fan of Roth's, however. (I was always more partial to his great rival, John Updike.) Of course I had read a number of his books, beginning with his breakout novella of 1959, *Goodbye Columbus*, when I was just a graduate student hoping to break out in my own way. After Roth's death, I heard an interview with him that had been conducted about ten years earlier in which he told a funny story about that book. He took his parents aside to warn them that the book would almost surely be controversial, and possibly a bestseller, so they should be prepared for attacks on their beloved son. His mother said nothing at the time, but years later Roth learned that afterward, she confided to her husband. "Oh, the poor boy. He has delusions of grandeur. He's bound to be disappointed."

And then about a decade later, Roth fulfilled his early promise by writing what is still his best-known novel, *Portnoy's Complaint*. And over the many years of his writing career, which didn't end until 2012, he churned out many books, mostly novels, and I read my share, I suppose. Offhand, I can think of his semi-autobiographical *Facts* (of course, many of Roth's books are autobiographical in nature), *The Human Stain, The Plot Against America*, and probably one or more of his Nathan Zuckerman novels – who can remember? I also read a lot *about* Roth who was naturally much written about. Especially damning was the memoir by his second wife, the actress Claire Bloom, who had her trials and grievances with Roth, a difficult and cranky man who prized his solitude. Not a good bet as a husband, and on that, in the end, Bloom lost.

But the book of his that is particularly germane here is one Roth wrote in 2006, when he was in his early 70s, after he had suffered a number of painful health crises and had begun to ponder what we all do if we live long enough – the horrors of old age and the terrifying specter of death. I use this phrase deliberately, not because I think of aging and death in these ways, but because Roth did.

The book I am referring to is his novella, *Everyman*, which is his meditation on disease, aging, diminishment, pain, loss, loneliness and death. On these subjects, his view is bleak and without hope or consolation. But before we turn to the story that Roth tells in this book in such a chilling way, it will be helpful if we take a brief glance at what Roth himself suffered during the course of his long life.

Actually, since I have not read a biography of Roth, I am not conversant with all of his physical woes, but David Remnick, the editor of The New Yorker, and a good friend, in a brief obituary gave us a quick summary. "He lived to be eighty-five, but he had little expectation of making it much past seventy. Over the years, there had been stretches of depression, surgeries on his back and spine, a quintuple bypass, and sixteen cardiac stents, which must be some kind of American League record." Claire Bloom also recounted some of Roth's other illnesses and surgeries, including occluded arteries and an unsuccessful operation on his knee. After that, he found himself in great pain, suffered from insomnia and nightmares and ultimately had a kind of crack-up, which Bloom ascribed to his use of the drug, Halcion, which was supposed to help him sleep but clearly had the opposite and a psychologically destabilizing effect. Of course Roth recovered in time. But it's clear that over the span of his life, he was no stranger to serious illnesses and many surgeries.

All this certainly colored the narrative line in *Everyman*, which tells the story, in the third person, of a nameless man (he is "everyman") retrospectively after his death. The book actually opens in a cemetery where he is being buried and toward the end Roth has him visiting his parents' grave in the same cemetery.

The book simply tells the story of this man's life from childhood to the expiration of his life. Talented as an artist, he winds up as an art director in an advertising agency and is quite successful in his career. He marries, has two sons, but finds himself constricted by the routines of marriage and drained by frequent quarrels with his wife, so he leaves them all behind and obtains a divorce. Later, he meets another woman whom he woes and wins, and they marry. After a blissful month's vacation with her, he becomes very ill and is in great pain from what turns out to be a burst appendix, which might have killed him were it not for its discovery at the last moment. But he recovers and lives a healthy life for over twenty years until he has another serious illness. This time it's his heart and it's again life-threatening. He has to endure a seven-hour surgery and undergoes a quintuple bypass operation. By now, he's on his third marriage, after having had a number of affairs, and finding himself alienated from his two boys. His third wife, a former model, is useless and his only close relationship is with his daughter, Nancy, from his second marriage. He will have seven more operations, usually heart-related, before his life comes to an end.

In the book, this man reflects on his life and, as he ages and becomes increasingly preoccupied with his own bodily decay and that of his friends, he finds himself ruing many of the choices he has made in his life. All the pain he has caused his wives, the loss of the affection and respect of his sons, his pointless affairs. Increasingly, wearied by disease, he becomes acutely lonely and clings, almost desperately, to the only person who has remained close to him, his daughter.

Some passages from the book will be helpful to illustrate not just this man's thoughts about the process of aging and the prospect of incipient death, but Roth's since he, too, is the everyman of whom he writes.

When toward the end of his life, he talks with several of his work colleagues who have become ill with serious diseases like those he has suffered, he thinks:

"Yet what he'd learned was nothing when measured against the inevitable onslaught that is the end of life. Had he been aware of the mortal suffering of every man and woman he happened to have known during all his years of professional life, of each one's painful story of regret and loss and stoicism, of fear and panic and isolation and dread, had he learned of every last thing they had parted with that had once been vitally theirs, and of how, systematically, they were being destroyed, he would have [realized that] …. Old age isn't a battle; old age is a massacre."

And he comes to see that he is in exactly the same condition as his colleagues:

"Now it appeared that like any number of the elderly, he was in the process of becoming less and less and would have to see his aimless days through to the end as no more than he was – the aimless days and uncertain nights and the impotently putting up with the physical deterioration and terminal sadness and the waiting and waiting for nothing."

The man now finds that his life has become pointless, without meaning, and comments, "All I've been doing is doodling away the time."

Roth has often spoken of his disdain for religion and its empty consolations, which he dismisses as superstitious fantasies unworthy of any intelligent and rational adult, and his character in this book feels the same way:

"Religion was a lie that he had recognized early in life, and he found all religions offensive, considered their superstitious folderol meaningless, childish, couldn't stand the complete unadultness – the baby talk and the righteousness and the sheep, the avid believers. No hocus-pocus about death and God or obsolete fantasies of heaven for him. There was only our bodies, born to live and die on terms decided by the bodies that had lived and died before us. If he could be said to have located a philosophical niche for himself, that was it."

He sums it all up in a tone of savage bitterness as one "who put no stock in an afterlife and knew without doubt that God was a fiction and this was the only life he'd have."

And this is how he goes to his death. This is the death of everyman.

It may surprise you to learn that when I read this book, there was much that I could identify with. I, too, had left wives – I had four – and had to leave two of my children behind. I have also spent a great deal of time (and wrote one entire confessional book on the subject) reflecting with considerable anguish on my wayward love life and the pain that it had brought to others. And like Roth's character, there have certainly been times in my life recently, during my "waiting to die" period, so to speak, that I have found myself aimless, seemingly just marking time. Particularly when suffering from chronic and painful conditions, I, too, became aware that I was in the midst of mourning the person I used to be who had already died.

Nevertheless, there are many and important differences between me and Roth's character. For one thing, I've been lucky, very lucky, that so far I have not had to endure any serious illnesses or undergo any of the kinds of surgeries that Roth or his character did. For another, I have always remained close to my children and am to this day. But the most important difference of course is my spiritual outlook on life, which was permanently affected by my first psychedelic experience when I was in my mid-thirties and was further deepened by my many years of working with near-death experiencers.

As a result, my view of death is exactly the opposite of Roth's. He is one of those Jewish intellectuals influenced by Freud and the tradition of psychoanalysis that was such a pervasive element in the intellectual lives of East Coast writers and artists who came to maturity during the middle part of the last century. I encountered many of them during my years of working in Connecticut and spending a lot of time in New York. For them, it's the familiar symbol of the grim reaper that represents death, a frightening image indeed. "Life is grim, and then you die." And after that, you disappear for good.

But I, a California Jew, who like Roth has no use for Judaism or any other religion, nevertheless find the teachings of the Buddha far more persuasive than those of Freud concerning how to view illness, decay and mortality. And of course, what has influenced me even more is my many conversations with near-death experiencers who have actually crossed the barrier between life and death, at least for a time, and who almost universally aver with the greatest certitude that there is indeed more to follow once death occurs. For them and for me the real symbol of death in our own time should be "the Being of Light." For Roth death is indeed a dead end. For those who have actually glimpsed beyond the veil, it is just the beginning of true life. For them, when death is encountered, it is not terrifying; instead it has the face of the Beloved.

Roth, an atheist, died in character, and for that we can admire him. But how many of us would really want to live as he did toward the end of his life – often shut up in his cabin chained to his writing desk and striving to hold the enemy, remorseless death, at bay as long as possible? Even after his "retirement" in 2012, he was seemingly unmoored and lost for a time when faced with the end of his career as an author: "I had reached the end. There was nothing more for me to write about. I was fearful I'd have nothing to do. I was terrified, in fact …." He did apparently manage to enjoy himself afterward for a while, but I still wonder, as I remarked at the outset, about the state of his mind when his waiting was finally over and he found himself face to face with death.

I like to think that maybe he was surprised at what he saw.

A necessary postscript: Just because Roth was an almost vehement atheist, I wouldn't want you to suppose that I am implying this is the way that most atheists live and approach death. Far from it. You can be an atheist and go gladly into death or at least without the crippling terror that death had for Roth. Think of David Hume, for example, who seemed to greet death joyfully and with humor. No, there is nothing about atheism *per se* that should make death difficult. But having some kind of spiritual perspective on life does help, and this is precisely what Roth and his everyman lacked. Fortunately, not all of us are that everyman. Roth will leave his legacy for those who are drawn to his view of life – and death. For my part, I choose to leave it, period.

In any case, as I've said, Roth's wait is over. I, on the other hand, am still waiting to die. But I am very far from being eager to approach my terminus. I hope there's still plenty of time before I shout "Can't wait!"

Nothing to Be Frightened Of

I should not really object to dying were it not followed by death.
— D. J. Enright
or perhaps Julian Barnes,
or was it Thomas Nagel? Possibly all three.

Dying is hard; death is easy.
Guess Who

For me, death is the one appalling fact that defines life; unless you are constantly aware of it, you cannot begin to understand what life's about. Only a couple of nights ago, there came again that alarmed and alarming moment, of being pitchforked back into consciousness, awake, alone, utterly alone, beating pillow with fist and shouting, "Oh no Oh no OH NO" in an endless wail, the horror of the moment. I say to myself, "Can't you face down death?" Can't you at least protest against it more interestingly than that? For God's sake, you're a writer; you do *words*. We know that extreme physical pain drives out language; it's dispiriting to learn that mental pain does the same.

No, that's not me talking. You should know that by now. Any guesses? The title of this essay should give you a hint since it's the title of a book he published about ten years ago.

OK, he's English. Primarily known as a novelist. Winner of the Man Booker Prize and many other literary honors.

Give up?

He's Julian Barnes, and he has a dread of death.

The account above, which I've condensed from the original, is just one example of what Barnes, who is an avid Francophile, likes to call *le réveil mortel* – an awakening with a sudden overwhelming terror of death.

I've been reading Barnes's novels on and off for years, beginning with one of his best-known early books, *Flaubert's Parrot*, of which I'm embarrassed to say I now remember nothing except that I was drawn to it by its intriguing title. But in recent years, I've returned to Barnes with pleasure and have read a number of his last spate of books, most of which strike a certain reflective elegiac tone. Among them, *The Sense of an Ending,* which is the book that was awarded the Man Booker Prize; *The Noise of Time,* a book based on some critical incidents in the life of the Russian composer, Dmitri Shostakovich; *Levels of Life,* a book in three parts that ends with a haunting and harrowing memoir of grief following the death of his wife, Pat Kavanagh; and, just now, another novel in three parts, *The Only Story.*

But the book I want to dwell on in this essay, one written just before the death of his wife and published in 2008, the very year of her death, is Barnes's meditation on death with the cunning title, *Nothing To Be Frightened Of.* On the contrary, however. As the book, at times unabashedly confessional but often laced with humor, makes clear, for most of Barnes's life, beginning when he was a young teenager, he has been obsessed with death and has come to dread it. For him, as he has remarked in more than one book, there is no God, no afterlife, only extinction and eternal nothingness. Just the inevitable passage toward this unspeakable abyss fills him with horror.

A friend asks him how often he thinks about death, and Barnes replies:

At least once each waking day ... and then there are the intermittent nocturnal attacks – what Barnes again calls *le réveil mortel* and goes on to elaborate with the help of a metaphor.

How to best to translate it? "The wake-up call to mortality" sounds a bit like a hotel service .... It is like being in an unfamiliar hotel room, where the alarm clock has been left on the previous occupant's setting, and at some ungodly hour you are suddenly pitched from sleep into darkness, panic and a vicious awareness that this is a rented world.

This is the sudden eruption of the terror of death, a kind of cosmic panic attack from which there is really no escape, only a temporary surcease until it recurs.

Writers seem to be particularly susceptible to such overwhelming frissons at the thought of death. Barnes recounts one such frightening incident in the life of Zola who seems to have been a particularly death-haunted person. Zola was part of a group of writers – all atheists or resolute agnostics – who used to meet at the Magny restaurant in Paris. It was a distinguished group that included, besides Zola, such literary eminences as Flaubert, Turgenev, Edmond de Goncourt and Alphonse Daudet.

In 1880, the year of Flaubert's death, when Zola was forty, *le réveil mortel* seems to have struck him with a shuddering impact. Zola was apparently unable to sleep and was gripped by what Barnes describes as "mortal terror." He later confessed all this to the remaining members of the Magny group, and Goncourt recorded it for his diary. Zola's confession and Flaubert's recent death got them all talking about death and eventually elicited a similar confession from Daudet about his own morbid obsessions about death.

Incidentally, there is an ironic coda concerning the death of Zola twenty years later. Zola was known to have imagined a kind of *belle mort* for himself where he would die in a sudden dramatic accident. He did in fact die in one, but not the kind he had envisioned for himself. He died of carbon monoxide poisoning in his bed.

This in fact is one of Barnes's great themes. He gives many examples of people imagining the way that they will die or would like to die, and then it turns out that their actual deaths are nothing like those suppositions and often take the form of a nasty surprise. As Barnes remarks:

> *"We shall probably die in hospital, you and I." A foolish thing to write, however statistically possible. The pace, as well as the place, of our dying is fortunately hidden from us. Expect one thing and you will likely get another.*

He then goes on to mention that the death of one of his favorite French authors, Jules Renard. When Renard turns forty-four, he thinks he may not double his years and die at eighty-eight. He was right, but his death came a lot sooner than he had imagined. By the next year, he could hardly walk and was dead at forty-six. Ya never know. Another reason that Barnes is spooked by death.

The poet Philip Larkin was still another writer who was pre-occupied with thoughts and fears about death – and what would come after. In one of his poems, he wrote these lines:

> Not to be here
> Not to be anywhere
> And soon; nothing more terrible, nothing more true

A biographer tells us that in his fifties, "the dread of oblivion darkened everything," and by his sixties, his fears became even more evident. Larkin himself wrote, "I don't think about death all the time, though I don't see why one shouldn't, just as you might expect a man in a condemned cell to think about the drop all the time. Why aren't I screaming?"

Larkin's own death was particularly and perhaps predictably ghastly. A friend visiting him the day before Larkin's death testified, "If Philip hadn't been drugged, he would have been raving. He was that frightened."

Barnes alludes to other famous writers whose psyches, likewise, were tormented by thoughts of death, including Kingsley Amis (whose early book, *Lucky Jim,* had me in stitches when I read it) and the poet, John Betjeman. Even the great Goethe, according to the doctor who attended him when he lay dying, went to his death "in the grip of a terrible fear and agitation."

Not content to frighten us by parading his roster of death-fearing writers before us, Barnes also devotes considerable attention to composers who were obvious "thanatophobes." Rachmaninov is a well-known exemplar of this condition, and Barnes aptly characterizes him as "a man both terrified of death, and terrified that he might survive afterward." Shostakovich is another familiar case. Among many other statements he made about death were these remarks: "Fear of death may be the most intense emotion of all. I sometimes think there is no deeper feeling."

As a kind of sidebar to give us a break from these morbid souls, as a lover of classical music myself and as one who has written a couple of books about classical composers, I couldn't help noticing how often Barnes would make references to them; they are strewn throughout his book. I eventually started making a list of them. Besides Rachmaninov and Shostakovich, Barnes alludes to Haydn, Mozart, Brahms, Ravel, Stravinsky, Rossini, Chabrier, Prokofiev and Bruckner – and I might have missed some!

He gives particular attention to Ravel because, I feel sure, what happened to him in his later years is especially tragic and horrifying. Which of course is just the sort of depressing grist that Barnes is keen to grind out to stoke our own fears of death.

As it happens, when I was writing about classical composers, I had read several books about Ravel, so I was already familiar with the story Barnes relates after Ravel began suffering from a form of cerebral atrophy during the last five or so years of his life. Believe me, you would wince in tearful sympathy to read it, so I will spare you the details. But toward the end, Ravel could no longer recognize his own music. At times this became almost comical and not just heartbreaking. After a performance of one of his pieces, the audience rose to salute him. But Ravel thought they were applauding the man next to him, so he joined in the applause.

(By the way, the same thing happened to Chabrier, who died of tertiary syphilis. He was also eventually unable to recognize the opera he had written – like Ravel, he thought it was the work of another composer.)

In a kind of macabre way, Barnes seems almost to relish narrating these stories, and there are far worse ones in his book, because he wants his readers to know how much can go wrong in our lives even before death, and why any sane person might well go nearly insane when it comes to thinking about death itself. "Nothing to be frightened of" indeed.

How did Barnes come to have the views he propounds in this book, as if to wake us from what we've been denying – the terrifying specter of death and the undeniable fact that it represents the absolute extinction of one's personality?

Barnes grew up in a non-religious home, and comments, almost with pride, that he was "never baptized, never sent to Sunday school [and that he has] never been to a normal church service in my life." His only sibling, a brother who became a philosopher, was likewise a non-believer and told Barnes that he had never "lost his faith" since he never had any and thought "it was a load of balls."

By the time he reaches Oxford, he tells the college chaplain that he is "a happy atheist," and, one gathers, so are most of his friends.

Once he becomes a well-known writer, his views about religion are pretty much set – "No God, no heaven, no afterlife," as he pithily puts it. And the writers he most admires – those from the past as well as the present – seem mainly to hew to a similar perspective, one in which God has no purchase. Barnes, too, comes to have his own Magny-like group, except it meets in Soho, and at the time of his writing his book on death, it is down to seven men, most in their sixties and seventies. When one night the conversation turns to a consideration of belief in an afterlife, "five and three-quarters" give it no credence, the fractional party calls religion a "cruel hoax," yet admits he "wouldn't mind if it were true."

This, then, is Barnes' intellectual milieu. The writers he honors are mostly from the same skeptical tribe and share the same mindset. This is his reference group; these are the people whose esteem he understandably cherishes. In a sense, they are the sorts of people he must have in mind when he writes his books.

So, naturally, he will make fun of and mock those who are religious and still believe, and seems to take delight in the fact that the great churches of England and Western Europe are these days mostly empty or just filled with tourists. After all, in a world after Darwin, Nietzsche and Freud had sent God packing, who can believe in this kind of superstitious crap any longer? It's unseemly.

And an afterlife? Barnes pokes fun at that too, as if to say, were he an American, "give me a *break!*" At one point in this connection, he refers to Arthur Koestler, who:

> *...before committing suicide, left a note in which he expressed "some timid hopes for a depersonalized afterlife."*
>
> *Such a view is unsurprising – Koestler had devoted many of his past years to parapsychology – but to me is distinctly unalluring. Just as there seems to be little point in a religion which is merely a weekly social event ... so I would want my afterlife, if one's on offer, to be an improvement – preferably a substantial one – on its terrestrial predecessor. I can just imagine slopping around half-unawares in some gooey molecular mix, but I can't see that this has any advantage over complete extinction. Why have hopes, even timid ones, for such a state?*

Barnes continues for another paragraph or two with more droll sarcasm of this kind, and he does seem to turn the idea of an afterlife into a complete absurdity. But here I have to interrupt where I want to take this essay for a moment to say that I am really being a bit unfair to Barnes. There is so much more in his book than I have indicated – a lot about his family, for example – that is witty, engaging, and wonderfully entertaining. He is a marvelous story-teller, as you would expect from a great novelist, which he is, and his book is full of memorable and amusing anecdotes (if you read it, be sure to look for the one about Rossini as an old lecher). But still....

But still, Barnes is woefully and perhaps willfully ignorant, it seems, about what has been happening for more than the last forty years in a world away from the one in which he has been immersed. I'm referring, of course, to all the research that has been done during that time on the near-death experience and similar phe-nomena. That research has given us an entirely new understanding of death (actually, it is a very old one; it's just been out of fashion for a long time) and is just one line of evidence, of several, that has made the case for survival of bodily death not only plausible, but almost impossible to deny. I submit that any person who is curious enough to examine this literature with an open mind will come to see that the accumulated body of evidence that has been amassed during this period clearly points to the conclusion that life is not a dead end and does not, as Barnes avers, end either in extinction or cosmic goo.

Ah, Julian, why don't you read my books since I have now read so many of yours? Something has happened since your Oxford days, and you haven't been paying attention. You might just have to reconsider some of your views!

Actually, Barnes might have already missed his chance when he was a young man. At that time, he was a journalist and one day came to interview an elderly novelist...

Then in his eighties, frail and bed-bound; death was not far away. At one point he picked up from his bedside table an anthology about immortality, and showed me a heavily underlined account of an out-of-body experience. This, he explained, was identical to one he had himself undergone as a soldier in the First World War. "I believe in resurrection," he said simply. I was awkwardly silent. "No, well, nor did I at your age," he went on sympathetically. "But I do now."

Barnes adds: "So perhaps I shall change my mind (though I doubt it)." Ken adds, "It's not too late, Julian!"

Well, of course, Barnes will never read these words and it's also doubtful that at his age – he is now 72 – he will start perusing the literature on NDEs, yet if he did, he would not only find evidence pointing to survival, but to the fact that as you enter through the portal of death, you take your personality with you, as NDErs attest. Let one example stand for many. One woman I interviewed told me that during her NDE, she found herself standing in a mist, "and I knew immediately that I had died and I was so happy that I had died, but I was still alive. And I cannot tell you how I felt. It was, 'Oh, God, I'm dead, but I'm here. I'm me!'" As the title of one recent book, which provides abundant documented evidence for the authenticity of NDEs, puts it, *The* Self *Does Not Die.*

And it's not just the research on NDEs that is giving us a new view of death. There's other research that is helping us to understand dementia in a new way, too. Barnes in his book relates some very distressing instances of people in demented states, and both of his parents eventually suffered debilitating strokes as well. Of course, these are the things we all dread and what makes the end of life for so many a fearful calamity, and yet it is not the whole picture. Consider, for example, the work on what is called "terminal lucidity."

It refers to a situation like this. Let's say you have an aged relative – let's make him your grandfather – who has had Alzheimer's for years during which time he has never been able to speak. Whoever he was seems to have disappeared leaving only the shell of his body. But then, astonishingly, shortly before his death, his eyes brighten, he is able to talk as lucidly as ever, and is able say how much he has always loved you, etc. He's clearly back in his full and familiar personality.

You are amazed and thrilled – but then, he becomes unconscious and not long afterward dies.

What to make of this? Was he there all along and just not able to break through until the end? How is such a thing possible when his brain has suffered irreversible damage?

You'd be surprised how often this sort of thing occurs, even though until recently there hasn't been much research on it. But I've been in touch with some of the leading researchers of terminal lucidity in this country and abroad and have a keen interest in their work. Heck, if I weren't pushing 83 and hampered by the trials of creeping decrepitude, that's what I'd be researching now!

One more piece of evidence that something entirely unexpected – and profoundly comforting and reassuring – can occur at the point of death. I am reminded of a line in Auden's long poem, "For the Time Being," that goes, "We who must die demand a miracle." Maybe terminal lucidity qualifies.

But returning to NDEs, I have saved the best news for last for all for people like Barnes who find themselves terrified by the thought of death. And here it is in a nutshell: *The greatest antidote to the fear of death, and what will quash it, is having an NDE!* Of course, not everyone can have an NDE, but as I point out in my book, *Lessons from the Light,* anyone who takes the trouble to look into and absorb the insights from NDEs can begin to reap for themselves many of their benefits, including the loss or sharp diminishment of the fear of death.

In any case, when I was first researching NDEs forty years ago, I collected testimonies from NDErs about the effects of their experience on their fear of death. Here's a small sampling of what they told me:

I had been terrified of death before, it [the NDE] left me with a total lack of fear of death.

Well, I certainly have no fear of death.

I'm not afraid of death at all.

I have no fear of death. I don't to this day.

If this is what death is like, then I'm not afraid to go .... I have absolutely no fear at all.

I have no fear of death.

I'm not afraid of dying. I'm really not afraid and I used to be scared to death.

I collected many such quotes from this research (but there is no point in endlessly listing them here) and all other NDE researchers have reported the same findings.

It's probably too late for Barnes to learn and take heart from these experiences, but presumably not for you, if you still find yourself fearful of death. Read the literature on NDEs, or better yet, talk to NDErs. It's one of the best ways I know to conquer the fear of death.

But all this, to be sure, doesn't fully address all aspects of Barnes's fear. Quite apart from the fear of death, what about the *fear of dying?*

Of course, NDEs don't do anything to diminish that. It's understandable to fear dying. If old age isn't for sissies, dying is surely not for the craven. Let's not kid ourselves; no one looks forward to dying (except those in extreme pain or those who are simply weary of life). And who knows what dying will be like for us? Who can say whether when the time comes, we will die "in character?" Elisabeth Kübler-Ross, the great expert on death, apparently had a very difficult time dying and was very angry. Who knows whether Ken Ring, the guy who spent half his life studying NDEs, won't die like Tolstoy's Ivan Illich by screaming for three days before his death? It's a crapshoot and you don't have the chance to load the dice.

Still, there's another way to look at this, and one that puts it in a more hopeful frame. Women know the pain of childbirth, but every person is eventually going to have to go into labor in order to jettison the body, to give it back. Women rightly fear childbirth; we all are right to fear dying. But afterward women have their babies and rejoice, and all of us who have to endure the possible agony of dying will be granted *a second birth* into a new life, which promises wonders of its own. Who would not look forward to that?

To end, perhaps you'll permit me a personal word, one that will allow me to come back full circle to the beginning of this essay and Barnes's *le réveil mortel.*

When I was a boy I rarely thought about death. Perhaps that was because no one close to me had died. Perhaps it was because I was not very imaginative. But I was not the kind of kid who would wake up during the night, terrified by the thought that one day I would die. So I never had my own *réveil mortel.* I was too busy thinking about baseball and girls to concern myself with the prospect of my death in the far distant future.

But now that I am well past eighty and waiting to die, I naturally think about death quite a lot. However, because I have been privileged to have talked to many hundreds, perhaps more than a thousand, near-death experiencers since 1977 during a long career as an NDE researcher and author, I no longer have any fear about death itself. Like virtually all NDErs who have lost their fear of death, mine has dissolved mainly because, I think, of my long immersion in near-death studies.

Instead of fear, I am ever more *curious* about what I will find when I die, assuming I ever get around to it. I have heard so many stories of what death is like. And I remember what Melville wrote about death's affording a last revelation that only "an author from the dead" could adequately tell." But what will *I* experience, if anything at all? That remains a mystery, a complete unknown. All my research concerning the experience of dying avails me no certainties about my own death. Life is an adventure, but the greatest adventure yet to come still lies ahead shrouded in darkness. But we know what follows darkness, don't we?

Love and Death

Those of you who are old enough may remember one of Woody Allen's early films with the title of this essay in which he stars with his then love, Diane Keaton, as a crazy 19th century Russian. But, never fear, this blog has nothing to do with that film or with Woody Allen, though it does have a tangential relationship with his first really great film, "Annie Hall", which came out in 1977. In that film, Woody, as the character, Alvy Singer, expresses his view of life in the form of one his quips: "I feel that life is divided into the horrible and the miserable," he tells her after which he recommends Ernest Becker's book *The Denial of Death* to Annie.

During those years in one of my courses at the University of Connecticut, I used Becker's book as a text to illustrate an existentialist view of life. In it, Becker argues that the fear of death, and our need to deny it, is fundamental to human existence: "The idea of death, the fear of it, haunts the human animal like nothing else; it is a mainspring of human activity – activity designed largely to avoid the fatality of death, to overcome it by denying in some way that it is the final destiny for man."

I mention this only to alert you to the fact that this essay will deal mainly with a man whose sensibility and view of life is quite similar to that of Woody Allen's and Becker's. Like them, this man throughout his life was spooked by a pervasive anxiety about death, but, perhaps surprisingly, he also had a tremendous capacity for love. It is a love story, then, that I want to relate, a story of love and death.

Irvin Yalom is a world-famous psychiatrist of distinctly existentialist persuasion, the author of about twenty books, some dealing with his work as a master therapist, others, revealing his gifts as a novelist. His books have sold millions of copies, and some of them have been translated into as many as thirty languages. And even in his late eighties, he continues to receive scads of e-mail and fan letters from his grateful readers, sometimes as many as forty a day. He's particularly well known for his novels about various philosophers, especially Nietzsche, Schopenhauer and Spinoza. I've read a couple of these myself, but the only one I still seem to have in my library is the one about Nietzsche, which is entitled *When Nietzsche Wept*. All in all, Yalom is an exceptional and accomplished human being. But to me, his greatest achievement has been as a lover.

The object of his amatory devotion was his wife, Marilyn, herself a distinguished scholar of French literature and feminist thought, and the author of about a dozen books. Like her husband, Marilyn was for a long time a professor at Stanford University and also for many years conducted literary salon in the Yaloms' home.

Irv Yalom, as I shall refer to him, though we've never met, is an introverted fellow, and as a youth he was shy and awkward, even on the dance floor, apparently having, like me, two left feet. He was bookish and a self-confessed nerd. Nevertheless, one night, when he was fifteen years old, he and a friend decided to crash a neighborhood party. But there was such a crush of people inside, they couldn't get in the front door. They had to climb through a window instead!

That night Irv experienced what the French call a *coup de foudre*. It occurred when he spotted the hostess, a fourteen-year-old girl. He was indeed thunderstruck, like a young John Gilbert first seeing Greta Garbo emerge from a carriage. I'll let Irv describe what happened that night:

> *Basically I'm not a highly social person [but] ... in the midst of a packed house, there was Marilyn, holding court.*

*I took one look at her and made my way through the crowd
to introduce myself to her. This was a highly unusual act on
my part: never before or after have I been so socially bold.
But it was indeed love at first sight. I phoned her the very
next day – my first phone call to a girl.*

Actually, it seems almost fated that they would meet and fall
in love. Consider the following uncanny "coincidences" in their
lives.

First, both Marilyn's father and Irv's emigrated to the United
States after World War II, each coming from small Jewish shtetls
(market towns) in Russia. Both happened to settle in Washington
D.C., where they both soon opened grocery stores. And, though
Irv and Marilyn only discovered this later, the stores were only
one block apart. Talk about propinquity! Irv muses about this in
the book:

*As a child and adolescent, I must have walked or biked past
my future father-in-law's store literally a thousand times!
Our fathers, though, never laid eyes on one another until
years after they retired and met at our engagement party.*

*Hence, from a distance, our early lives seem similar:
parents who emigrated from Eastern Europe, fathers who
had grocery stores only a block from one another.*

If any of you happen to be familiar with the writings of the
famous novelist, Vladimir Nabokov, this story may ring a bell.
Here's why: Nabokov developed a theory of fate based on his
own experience with his wife, Véra, with whom he had a long and
fruitful marriage. They both grew up in privileged circumstances
in pre-revolutionary Russia. After the revolution, both families
fled, first, to Crimea, as I recall, and after that, to Paris, and then
to Berlin (I may have the order of these places confused, but that
doesn't really matter). In any event, Nabokov eventually discovered that their families had moved in the same circles in each

location, but somehow Vladimir and Véra never chanced to meet each other. Finally, in Berlin, they found themselves at a masked ball and guess what? Kismet!

From this experience, Nabokov formulated his theory of fate. In essence, it says that "the powers of Eros" meant for these two to meet and kept arranging circumstances so that eventually what was destined to happen, would. Like God, love works in mysterious ways.

In any case, like the Nabokovs, the Yaloms have been together ever since the night of that party. She was in his one and only. After they both completed their professional training, they got married and went on to enjoy a sixty-five-year-long love affair. Eventually, they had four very talented children (and eight grandchildren), and both of them had very successful professional careers and gobs of wonderful friends and colleagues. Their house, thanks largely to Marilyn's outgoing nature and grace, became the center for years of lively gatherings and parties. In many ways, the Yaloms were blessed with the best of everything a couple could wish for.

Until 2019 when Marilyn turned out to have developed multiple myeloma, a cancer of the plasma cells. Chemotherapy followed, but it led to a stroke, and more time in the hospital. Marilyn recovered pretty well from the stroke, but she would never recover from her cancer.

Obviously, this was devastating to them both, but Marilyn had an idea that she thought would help them cope with it. She did not merely propose, but insisted, that they finally write a book together about how they both would deal with her illness. They would each write alternate chapters. And so they did. The book is called *A Matter of Death and Life,* and I've just finished reading it.

Marilyn didn't live long enough to complete it. She lived only about six months before dying shortly before Thanksgiving in 2019. The book is really divided in another way, not just in having two authors. The first and longest part of the book is really a love story, one of the most moving I have ever read. The last third of the book is Irv's alone where he writes about his anguished bereavement following Marilyn's death. That part was almost unbearable for me to read. But what I want to write about in this essay is mostly their love story. It's Irv's love for and devotion to his wife that makes this book so immensely emotionally powerful.

Listen to how Irv writes about her in August when Marilyn has only a few months left to live (though neither of them knows that yet):

> *Marilyn and I spend the rest of the day close together: my first impulse is not to let her out of my sight, to stay near, to hold her hand and not let it go. I fell in love with her seventy-three years ago, and we have just celebrated our sixty-fifth wedding anniversary. I know it is unusual to adore another person so much and for so long. But, even now, whenever she enters the room, I light up. I admire everything about her – her grace, her beauty, her kindness, and her wisdom.*

Later, after Marilyn dies, he reiterates how strong his love was for her: "I never doubt the depth of my love for Marilyn. I feel certain that no man has ever loved a woman more." And reading this book, you don't doubt it either. He spends endless time with her – hour after hour – while she gets her chemo or other forms of treatment. They hold hands constantly – they always have – and remain as physically close as possible. He takes incredibly good and loving care of her. His every gesture toward her bespeaks his ardent love. And he desperately doesn't want her to die. He can't stand the thought of being without her.

And here we have to change the focus from the terrible suffering that Marilyn is to undergo during the course of her illness with which much of the first part of the book is concerned to Irv's own problems, which are considerable.

For one thing, he has recently had to deal with a pacemaker. But worse, he has serious problems with his balance and has to use a cane and a walker in order to avoid the possible calamity of a fall. He no longer feels comfortable driving either. But most troubling of all is that his memory is starting to fail. He can no longer remember some of the books he's written or call up the faces of some of his patients he treated for years or recognize the actors in the television series that he and Marilyn love watching together. Throughout the book, he worries about this because Marilyn, whose memory is excellent, has become the repository of many of Irv's memories. When she dies, those memories, which help to structure his sense of identity, will be lost forever. Her death will be like a partial amputation of his self. In a sense, that part of him will die with her. And because he has a dread of dementia, too, this is terrifying to him.

After she dies, he writes a letter to his wife in which he gives voice to these fears:

So many times, Marilyn, I search my memory in vain – I think of someone we met, some trip we took, some play we saw, some restaurant we dined at – but all these happenings have vanished from my memory. Not only have I lost you, the most precious person to me in the world, but so much of my past has vanished with you. My prediction that, when you left me, you would be taking with you a good part of my past has proved to be true.

As you read through this book, you come to understand that because of the very strength of Irv's love for Marilyn, there develops a terrible struggle between them. Marilyn feels so wretched so much of the time, she longs to die, but Irv just longs for her – longs for her to remain alive, not to leave him. There are several passages in the book where she begs him to let her go while he entreats her not to die. "How much longer must I live before I am allowed to die," she cries. "If I could place you inside my body for just a few moments, you would understand." But Irv, after a long moment of silence, is immune to Marilyn's plea to be released. He counters: "Isn't it enough that you are still alive? That when you go, there will be nothing afterward. And I'm not ready to let you go."

Later, Irv is sobbing and says, "I cannot bear the thought of your dying. I cannot cope with the thought of living in a world without you." To which Marilyn replies:

> *Irv, don't forget I've been living in pain and misery for ten months now. I've said to you again and again that I cannot bear the thought of living like this any longer. I welcome death .... Irv, it's time. Please you've got to let me go.*

Impasse.

Their battle over who is in control of Marilyn's life reveals the dark side of love, which is attachment. Marilyn is ready to let go, Irv cannot. He is too attached to her, too entwined. He feels he will die without her or at least will not want to live. Attachment is a killer. But if you live long enough, you will eventually lose everything and everyone you have loved. And ultimately yourself. Letting go is the great lesson in life. Marilyn understands this; Irv is too attached to Marilyn even to hear it much less to heed this dictum.

But there's something else that impedes Irv's acceptance of Marilyn's entreaties. As he confesses at many points in the book, he has suffered for much of his life from death anxiety. He even spent a couple of years working with the celebrated existential psychologist, Rollo May, to deal with this issue. But it was unsuccessful – he was still fearful of death. Another instance of his inability to let go. Clinging to life is not a recipe for well being for anyone facing death, his own or that of a loved one.

Both Marilyn and Irv were atheists, but Marilyn herself was not afraid of death.

> *The idea of death does not frighten me. I do not believe in an afterlife beyond a "reintegration into the cosmos," and I can accept the idea that I shall no longer exist.*

Irv's atheism, however, was more militant. He became an atheist at the age of thirteen, he remarks, and like many Jewish intellectuals, the idea of an afterlife for him was both irrational and preposterous.

I've always scoffed at irrational thinking, at all the mystical notions about heaven and hell and what happens after death ... Rationality and clarity are major reasons why my books are used in classrooms around the world.

I wonder whether Irv had even heard of NDEs. If he did, he surely wouldn't have given them any credence.

In the end, it didn't matter what either Marilyn and Irv believed. Marilyn's situation became increasingly unbearable to her and ultimately she chose hospice care and elected to have physician-assisted suicide. Irv stayed with her to the last, holding her hand and weeping.

My head is next to Marilyn's head, and my attention riveted on her breathing. I watch her every movement and silently count her breaths. After her fourteenth feeble breath, she breathes no more.

I lean over to kiss her forehead. Her flesh is already cool: death has arrived.

My Marilyn, my darling Marilyn, was no more.

Love and death.

∽

There is so much more in this book than I have had the space to describe. Indeed, I have only sketched the barest outlines of the love story of Irv and Marilyn. It is so much more richly textured and nuanced than my account will have suggested. Plus, their lives, interests and accomplishments are fascinating in themselves. And of course, as I earlier indicated, I have said almost nothing about the very heartrending grief that Irv describes following Marilyn's death.

Also, a fuller narrative would have included a discussion of issues having to do with the right to die movement, but I elided those in part because I will discuss this topic in a subsequent essay. At least Marilyn was able to avail herself of physician-assisted suicide, which is legal in California, but still difficult because of its strict requirements.

I can only urge my readers to get ahold of this beautiful book. It is a love story as deeply affecting as anything I have read in a long time.

After reading the book, I checked the Internet and discovered to my surprise that Irvin Yalom is still alive at 90, which makes him the longest-lived member of his family. He did not think he would long survive Marilyn's death, but, obviously, he has.

In the book, he tells her that he wished that after she was buried, he could be buried with her in the same coffin when his time came. He knew that was impossible, but he couldn't stand the thought of being separated from her.

But if I could speak to Irv, I think I would want to say something like this:

Dear Irv,
Death is not a wall, it's a curtain. When your time comes, just pull back that curtain and jump through the window. She'll be there waiting for you.

We are never really separated from those to whom we truly belong. Their absence is only apparent and temporary. When you leave the temporal world behind to enter eternity, Marilyn will be there to greet you and you will be able hold her hand once again.

What About Animals?

Do Our Pets Have an Afterlife?

We all know what happens when we die – we don't.

At least that's what most of us believe, whether by religious faith or because we've been convinced by the collective testimony of near-death experiencers or perhaps for other reasons. But whatever the basis of our beliefs, we hold that life isn't a dead end. Upon death, we just continue to exist in another form.

But what about our pets? The philosopher, Martin Heidegger, argued that animals don't die; they simply disappear, he said.

But do they? Are they so unlike us – creatures without a soul, according to Descartes – that upon their physical death, they simply cease to exist?

Don't be too sure. Let's look at the evidence first before we reluctantly consign our pets to perpetual oblivion.

Janice Holden is the current President of The International Association for Near-Death Studies, an organization I co-founded more than forty years ago, and the longtime editor of *The Journal of Near-Death Studies*. She is certainly a recognized authority on NDEs. In a recent interview, she asserted that although she was unaware of any systematic research dealing with the perception of pets during NDEs, nevertheless, there are "numerous reports that people were reunited with beloved deceased pets during their NDEs." I have also been assured by P.M.H. Atwater, another well-known NDE researcher, that it is not just dogs and cats that are perceived by NDErs, but pet birds as well.

Here, however, we will focus just on cats and dogs. And for

this purpose, we can draw on the work of Jeff Long, another prominent NDE researcher. Jeff also hosts the most important and widely regarded NDE website, The Near-Death Experience Research Foundation (or NDERF), and has collected quite a few cases of this kind. Let's now just consider several of those in his files.

I will not take the space here to quote the entirety of these NDE reports or give the circumstances of their occurrence. Instead, I will just quote the relevant portions concerning their perception of deceased pets.

Michael

As I raised my head up from the ground to look around, I saw my deceased dog from my childhood bounding towards me. I remember exclaiming her name at the top of my lungs as I saw her bounding towards me. It was overwhelmingly wonderful. I felt completely at peace and totally happy. I was so excited to see her again, and I did not question the experience at the time. It was as if she had never died and she had always been waiting for me to wake up from my nap in the grass. The thought 'why is my dead dog here?' never occurred to me. The thought 'where am I and why am I laying in this field of grass?' never occurred to me. Everything was simply as it was supposed to be.

The experience was very brief, but VERY real. An entire reality was just as real as our world is now. There was not a single aspect of that experience which did not feel real.

Tracy

A dog's tail weaved through the tall grass. A beautiful fuzzy puppy wagged her tail at me. At first, I did not recognize her. I had never seen our dog as a puppy. I was so happy to see her. We had to put her down two weeks prior to my daughter's birth. She had injured her hip. We had given all the surgery we could to keep her, but it did not make her quality of life better – it had become much worse. *We had her put down on my due date. Our hearts were so heavy with the loss of the dog that generously shared her life with us for 12 years.*

Kustav

I saw a piece of floating land in the distance. It had one pine tree and covered in snow. I was still so cold, but decided to go to that tree. Below the tree, I heard a meow. I looked down, and saw Elmar! Elmar was a white Persian cat. I could not believe it. He was watching me. His beautiful green eyes and long, luscious white fur. Suddenly, I realized I had hands. I was surprised by this. I picked up Elmar. While I held him, he purred. No longer did I feel cold. His fur completely warmed me up and I felt the energy of his love. It was just like old times. I began to cry in feeling of happiness. I could even smell him exactly the way he used to smell. I put him down, and could tell from his purring and rubbing up against me that I would be o.k., whether that meant returning to life or staying on this floating Island. Then, I realized Elmar's eyes had the same look as I remembered when something got his attention.

Wayne

There was a Boston Terrier dog standing beside her. We had always had Boston Terriers as pets when I was a kid but I didn't recognize this particular dog.

As a side-note, I went through a big box of old family photos and I found the dog with my grandmother. Her name was Trixie and she was our household pet when I was born in 1956. I don't remember her though as she was put to sleep around 1958. It was definitely, absolutely Trixie with my grandma.

Jonathan

I then became distracted by figures to my right which were all my former pets (dogs and cats that had died) climbing over each other to get to me, they gave me the impression of me just getting home from a long trip as they seemed very excited to see me.

Yvette

I'm in a park. Green grass was everywhere. It was very pretty and very clean. I see a black cat running up to me. It's my Amigo, my black cat who had passed away 6 months earlier. He runs towards me and leaps into my arms. He feels exactly the same. He was always a solid cat from his years on the streets. I hold him tight; I am so happy to see him. Joy fills me!! I cry a little bit. I hold him, hugging him, kissing him. He's rubbing his cheek on my face. I am so happy to see him. He is so happy to see me. This happiness is as if I've never felt before. I could feel his love and adoration. I have never felt happiness like this before in my life. It was peaceful, comforting, and so fulfilling.

Scott Janssen is a hospice social worker who has also reported cases of this kind in a recent article on this subject, "Near Death Experiences: Will Our Dogs be Waiting For us?" Here is just one such case.

Alma

I remember leaving my body. I could see myself on the ground below and the ambulance guys working on me. It was all very strange. Then I felt myself moving away. I saw a beautiful light and heard this amazing music that just brought me such peace. Eventually I found myself in a big yard where I'd grown up. I saw Sadie, my best childhood friend, a cute little Schnauzer. She was running toward me, wagging her tail. I'd missed her so much when she died. Yet, there she was, coming to greet me. She was licking me like crazy and I was laughing with joy.

I don't need to adduce more such stories, do I, in order to establish the answer to my question. Yes, Virginia, our pets truly do seem to have an afterlife.

But do our pets *really* live after they die? Perhaps they are just figments of our desires and we simply hallucinate them once we ourselves pass over to the life beyond this one.

Well, consider: Reports of NDEs often involve the perception of loved ones who appear to greet us when we pass over. You might argue that we hallucinate them, too, but hold on. Not so fast with your skepticism.

What about those cases, and there are more than a few, when an individual is greeted by someone she doesn't know or recognize, only to be told afterward that that was your grandfather (who died before you were born and whom you never knew). Or say a person returns from an NDE and reports that he was greeted by his sister – only he never had a sister. Except that his mother now tells him what he never knew. He had a sister but she died at the age of two before he was born. Or suppose you see someone during your NDE whom you know still to be alive, only to find that he died three days before when you were ill, and so forth.

No, we are typically greeted by those who have formed a deep bond with us or we with them. And isn't it true that we often have formed a very deep bond with our pets and they with us? Why shouldn't those bonds also prevail after death, just as they do with the people we have loved and been attached to?

The bonds we form with our pets in life are not severed by their death. Our separation from them is only temporary. If we can trust these accounts of pets observed during NDEs, it means that we will indeed be reunited with them after we die. And for any animal lover, what could bring greater joy than to see our beloved cat or dog once more to greet us when we pass over?

Facing Death

Better Dying Through Chemistry

A high dose psychedelic experience is death practice.
— Katherine McLean, psychedelic therapist

Lately, I've been reading a new book by the celebrated food guru, Michael Pollan, the author of *The Omnivore's Dilemma* and other well-known books about food and the food industry. But his new book isn't about food. It's all about psychedelic drugs, and its subtitle tells you exactly what Pollan is on to in this surprising turn in his professional career: *What the New Science of Psychedelics Teaches Us About Consciousness, Dying, Addiction, Depression, and Transcendence.* Wow, about the only thing he left out is the proverbial kitchen sink.

Well, did you *know* that there is such a thing as a "new science of psychedelics?" Indeed there is, and if you haven't noticed, it's actually been going on for the last two decades. And these days it's legit, too, with research programs being carried out by distinguished scholars and academics at some of the leading universities in the U.S. as well as in Europe. Pollan's bestselling book, entitled *How to Change Your Mind,* is an excellent journalistic account of all this work and what we can all learn from it, regardless of whether we have used psychedelics or not.

For me personally, however, it is also a remembrance of trips past because psychedelics were once a pivotal part of my life, and before picking up Pollan's book I was already personally familiar with many of the figures who played an important part in this movement in the days before its recent and surprising re-emergence as an exciting and thriving area of research into the mysteries of consciousness. Yes, indeed, I, too, had my adventures as a psychonaut back in the day, and this book revived many of those memories....

In these essays, I usually try to stay pretty much in the present tense, and before concluding it I will return there, but to set the stage for what I really want to end up discussing – which *is* our end – I hope you will indulge me for a few moments so that I can describe my own improbable and unplanned entry into a world I had no clue even existed. What I am about to relate was, in fact, the most important thing that ever happened to me, and after it my life was never the same.

In March of 1971, when my then wife and I went off to the Berkshires to celebrate our anniversary, I happened to pick up a book that she was then reading – Carlos Castañeda's first book, *The Teachings of Don Juan.* It looked intriguing and after she had finished it, I read it.

I was then a typical Jewish professor – wedded to rational thought, committed to science and atheistic in my worldview. I had no interest in religion and very little knowledge of mysticism. But I was open to new experiences, and what had particularly excited me about Casteñeda's book was his discussion of what he called "seeing the crack between the worlds," which he had apparently effected through the use of mescaline.

At the time, I had never considered using psychedelic drugs and my only familiarity with anything close was having smoked marijuana a few times. But since I had never been a smoker, even that was difficult for me, and my experiences with it, though of the usual kind, did not have any particular impact on my life.

Nevertheless, since there was a long-haired hippie-ish colleague in my department at the time who I knew was familiar with psychedelics, I approached him to tell him about my interest to take mescaline and why. This fellow was one of those half-crazy/

half genius types that most of my colleagues had no use for but whose brilliance and charisma were enough of a compensation to keep him on the faculty. In any case, he had read Castañeda's book and knew what I was after.

I came to the point. Could he provide me with some mescaline? He could.

By then it was early May. The semester was just about over. He told me not to read anything further on the subject and just come to his apartment on the following Saturday.

That day turned out to be a rare beautiful sun-splashed day with everything beginning to bloom. My colleague lived at the edge of a forest. He suggested that I take the mescaline in his apartment, wait just a bit and listen to music and then go outside into the nearby woods.

And then he gave me two purple pills to ingest.

I did not know my colleague well, and as I was soon to find out, he was not only impish, but embodied the trickster archetype. While he gave me to believe I was taking mescaline, he had actually given me 300 micrograms of LSD, a very high dose.

I will not bore you with an account of the next twelve hours. Suffice it to say that all the pillars of my previous ontological categories soon began to crumble into dust. At the time and afterward I realized that this was the most important and most transformative experience of my life – and more than fifty years later, I still feel the same way. I had the undeniable feeling that I was seeing the world as it really was with pristine eyes for the first time. And once I did, I could never return to the person I had been for he, too, had been obliterated.

The one portion of the experience I will allude to here – because it eventually led me to the study of near-death experiences – took place when I was sitting on a log near a stream in the woods. I don't know how long I was there, but at some point for a moment outside of time I – except there was no "I" any longer – experienced an inrushing of the most intense and overwhelming rapturous LOVE and knew instantly that this was the real world, that the universe, if I can put this way, was stitched in the fabric of this love, and that I was home. However, again I have to repeat: There was *only* this energy of love and "I" was an indissoluble part of it, not separate from it.

In fact, I was soon to learn that this experience of "non-duality" in which one becomes aware of the primacy of love is fairly common in psychedelic journeys, and Pollan himself had a similar experience the first time *he* took LSD and comments, as all psychedelic voyagers will attest, at the paucity and seeming banality of using everyday words to describe the ineffable:

Platitudes that wouldn't seem out of place on a Hallmark card glow with the force of revealed truth.

Love is everything.

Okay, but what else did you learn?

No – you must not have heard me; it's **every**thing.

Pollan also mentions that Aldous Huxley had the same insight the first time *he* was given LSD:

What came through ... was the realization ... of Love as the primary and fundamental cosmic fact .... The words, of course, have a kind of indecency and must necessarily ring false, seem like twaddle. But the fact remains.

And again, in interviewing another psychedelic sojourner, who will allude to where we are going with this, Pollan hears her say: *I remember thinking, if this is death, I'm fine with it. It was ... bliss. I had the feeling, no, the* knowledge – *that every single thing there is is made of love.*

This indeed is the exact same revelation that comes to people who have actually experienced the first stages of physical death when they undergo an NDE. Let the following example, which I draw from my book, *Lessons from the Light,* stand for the many accounts of NDEs I have heard over my more than forty years researching such experiences. This woman was writing of her encounter with a being of light:

> *...the light told me that everything was Love, and I mean everything .... I vividly recall the part where the light did what felt like switch on a current of pure, undiluted, concentrated unconditional LOVE. This love I experienced in the light was so powerful it can't be compared to earthly love .... It's like knowing that the very best love you feel on earth is diluted to about one part per million of the real thing.*

Which brings up a question: If psychedelics can afford direct knowledge of the primacy of love in such an overwhelming way, and if near-death experiencers encounter the same truth when they come close to death, then might it be possible to use psychedelics with terminally ill people to afford them a preview of what they may actually encounter when they die?

> He who dies before he dies
> Does not die when he dies.
> — Angelus Siliseus
> 1624-1677

Ketamine is a dissociative anesthetic, which when used at sub-anesthetic levels induces a very distinctive but powerful alteration in consciousness that some people feel mimics the experience of death. In 1984, I was asked by a psychedelic therapist whether I would be willing to participate in a study she was carrying out with an oncologist to determine whether ketamine did induce something like an NDE. (Presumably, I was being tapped for this study because I was an "expert" in such matters – despite never having had an NDE myself.) The idea was that since NDEs almost always cause a loss of the fear of death, ketamine might serve a similar purpose for those facing imminent death, such as terminally ill cancer patients.

I eventually did accept the offer and wound up taking it a number of times. I have written about my ketamine experiences elsewhere (those interested will find my account in a book called *The Ketamine Papers,* edited by Phil Wolfson and Glenn Hartelius), and although I personally did not find that they resembled very closely NDEs, others have reported striking similarities. And, indeed, since my own adventures with ketamine, there have been some very promising preliminary case studies reported in which ketamine has significantly reduced fear of death in cancer patients.

Furthermore, beginning in 1965 and continuing into the next decade, the psychiatrist and leading psychedelic therapist, Stanislav Grof, and his colleagues at Spring Grove Hospital in Baltimore, using LSD with terminally ill patients reported the same thing and many other benefits as well in a significant number of cases.

Finally, Michael Pollan brings us up to date in his book with the latest studies of this kind using psilocybin. Preliminary but very impressive studies have been conducted at both NYU and Johns Hopkins, and once again, 80% of terminally ill cancer patients "showed clinically significant reductions in standard measures of anxiety and depression, an effect that endured for at least six months after their psilocybin session." Moreover, the patients with the best outcomes were precisely those who themselves had had the most complete mystical experiences, presumably akin to an NDE.

These findings astounded even the researchers carrying out these studies. One of then confessed, "I thought the first ten or twenty people were plants – that they must be faking it. They were saying things like 'I understand love is the most powerful force on the planet'…. People who had been palpably scared of death – they lost their fear. The fact that a drug given once could have such an effect for so long is an unprecedented finding. We have never seen anything like that in the psychiatric field."

But lest this essay become too academic, let me simply quote a couple of brief excerpts from these patients. First, from a man named Patrick who had these insights during his psilocybin session: *"From here on, love was the only consideration ... It was and is the only purpose. Love seemed to emanate from a single point of light.... I could feel my physical body trying to vibrate in unity with the cosmos."* Aloud he said, "Never had an orgasm of the soul before." And then later, "It was right there in front of me ... love ... the only thing that mattered."

Next, from Dinah, who described herself to Pollan as a "solid atheist." Nevertheless, Pollan relates that in her psilocybin-induced epiphany, she experienced feelings of "overwhelming love," and later said that she felt herself "bathed in God's love." When Pollan pointed out that using such a phrase would seem to be in contradiction to her professed atheism, she retorted, "What other way is there to express it?"

So from all this, we have learned that psychedelics can be very effective for the terminally ill in helping them overcome the fear of death and their depression about dying, thus enabling them to die with greater serenity and peace of mind. But what about a more radical possibility?

How about administering LSD, *at the very point of death*, so that one goes out riding high on the wave of a psychedelically-induced ecstasy?

Actually, it's been done, and no less by than Aldous Huxley himself whose second wife, Laura, administered LSD to him on his deathbed while urging him to "go toward the light." She has said that he died with "a very beautiful expression on his face." (By an odd stroke of fate, he was having his drug-aided death experience that same day, November 22, 1963, that John Kennedy was assassinated.)

Which as promised brings us back, at last, to the present moment that finds me still waiting for death and thinking again about psychedelics. I'm wondering whether I should follow Huxley and die with the aid of a psychedelic agent when my time comes. If it comes.

Check with me later.

Or just read my obit.

The Last Dance

Half a lifetime ago – I was in the summer of my life then – I was running the newly formed International Association for Near-Death Studies (IANDS) at the University of Connecticut. It was at that time that I became acquainted with a then noted anthropologist named Virginia Hine who was one of the first persons to become a member of this organization. We hit it off immediately and soon became good, even loving, friends.

I had actually heard of Ginny before she joined IANDS. I had read one of her articles on altered states of consciousness, which had impressed me, and a bit later, her book, *Last Letter to the Pebble People,* which dealt with the death of her beloved husband, Aldie, of cancer a few years earlier.

Over the years, our letters grew warm and loving despite the fact that we were never able to meet. She mostly divided her time between her home in Florida and her organization, Rites of Passage, in California. Whenever I traveled to Florida, she seemed to be in California, and vice versa. Once, when she came to Connecticut, I was away myself. We came to joke about our mismatched schedules. The closest we ever came to meeting face to face was a single telephone call. I remember that she had a beautiful voice.

When one day I received a letter from Ginny informing me that she had decided to choose the manner and time of her death, and that the time was coming quite soon, I was stunned. I had not known or suspected her plans. I remember thinking, "Now we will never meet!"

I thought a good deal about that letter of hers before replying to it. I could see that she had considered the matter extremely carefully and that she had discussed her plans thoroughly with her friends and family. She had secured some Seconal, which she knew would allow her to die peacefully, which according to her family, as I was to learn later, had indeed proved to be the case.

She did not need nor did she ask for any advice from me. I certainly did not attempt to dissuade her – it was her choice, and I respected that. I knew she had been ill with cancer and in pain. In the end, I could only send her my love and prayers for a gentle passage into death. I also didn't think that it made sense to regard Ginny's death as a suicide. Instead, I viewed it as an example of a well-planned and rational *chosen death*.

I had occasion to think of Ginny recently as a result of reading a new book by a journalist named Katie Englehart entitled *The Inevitable: Dispatches on the Right to Die.* It is full of cases like that of Ginny's. These days, many people are choosing to die the way Ginny did, and an increasing number of them are doing so by finding ways to circumvent the law.

Frankly, if you will indulge a brief confessional aside, now that I'm in the deep winter of my life, I have to admit that in recent years, I've thought quite a bit about the fact that I definitely do *not* want to wind up, decrepit and demented, in one of those warehouses for the those slated for death that we euphemistically call "nursing homes." No sirree, that's not for me! After all, would anyone, given the choice, opt to spend their last years in such a depressing environment surrounded by scores of wheelchair-bound human wrecks just "waiting to die," to use the title of one of my recent immortal books?

I have a couple of friends who share my concern about these end-of-life matters, and we have had a number of conversations over the years about how best to dispatch ourselves. A few years ago, for example, we all read and discussed Derek Humphry's 1991 best seller, *Final Exit,* which describes various ways to kill yourself (the book has sold over two million copies in twelve languages). I did not find any of the methods Humphry offers particularly appealing nor did my friends, but one of them has since made plans to lay in a supply of drugs that she feels would do the job for her. The three of us don't exactly have a "pact" with each other about how to prepare for a self-administered exit, should one become necessary, but we have certainly explored a number of options.

Englehart, however, has encountered people who have made such a pact. In fact her book begins with such an example. She had interviewed a New Yorker whom she calls Betty who had made such a pact with her two best friends. "We have a pact," Betty told Englehart. "The first one who gets Alzheimer's gets the Nembutal."

Although Betty herself was in good health in her seventies, she had been around a number of even older people, including one man in his nineties, and was distressed to see them in deep pain and just "hanging around," to use her phrase. But worst was having to witness her husband die.

Her own husband had died quickly enough. Seventy-five years old. Cancer. Still, he suffered. Sometimes he cried. In his final days, Betty imagined taking firm hold of a pillow and smothering him, partly because she thought that's what he would have wanted, but also because she couldn't bear to see him that way. In the end, he grew so agitated that the doctors gave him enough painkillers to knock him out. He spent three days in a morphine-induced languor and then died. Betty and her friends agreed that they would never let themselves get to that place and also they would never rely on a physician to help them, because who knew where the bounds of a doctor's mercy lay?

(Incidentally, Betty's account here reminded me of Michael Haneke's marvelous and moving 2012 film, "Amour," in which an elderly husband eventually has to suffocate his demented wife with a pillow because he was unable to bear her suffering any longer.)

Betty wound up going to Mexico where she had learned she could buy in pet stores a lethal poison that is used to euthanize dogs. She was able to score enough for her and her friends. The story of her escapade is actually quite amusing and was not without risk, but you'll have to read the book for that. However, the point is that in New York, physician-assisted death is still illegal. If you wanted to orchestrate your own death, it had to be a DIY endeavor.

Actually, in the book, Englehart doesn't spend much time talking about people like Betty. Instead, she focuses on those who have serious, debilitating and often very painful illnesses, and who are often desperate to die, but who do not qualify for physician-assisted death even in the states where it is legal. She also spends a great deal of time interviewing doctors, nurses, researchers, authors, advocates for and opponents of the right-to-die movement. In each of her six chapters, she focuses on one personal story: two about doctors who specialize in helping people to die and four case studies of people who wanted to die because of unbearable suffering they were forced to endure. One because she had lived too long and nothing worked anymore; one who was suffering from multiple sclerosis; another who had progressive dementia; and a fourth who was mad.

Engelhart is herself not an advocate for the rights of the dying; she is a reporter who simply narrates these stories and who tries to listen to them without judgment but with compassion. She is open to a variety of perspectives. Self-administered death, like abortion, is a controversial subject. But when you read the heartbreaking stories of those who do not "qualify" to die because they do not satisfy the eligibility requirements, such as having been certified as being "within six weeks of dying" or for other reasons, it's impossible not to feel sympathy for those who find themselves having to operate outside the law in order to effectuate their own deaths. It's like reading what pregnant women had to go through or still do where abortion is illegal. *The Inevitable* is one long horror story. But it is also the story of some very courageous physicians who have risked everything in order to help such people.

One of themes that runs through Englehart's book – it almost becomes a cliché or a tired trope – is how many people yearning to die because of their needless suffering often mention that we euthanize our dogs and cats in a loving way. One man, at a conference on death with dignity, sported a t-shirt saying, "I want to die like a dog." Does it make sense that we can compassionately end the suffering of our beloved pets but can't extend the same mercy to ourselves? After all, we didn't really need Darwin to tell us that we are animals, too.

Recently I was reading an article about all the horses who died a couple of years ago at the track at Santa Anita – 37 of them in 2019, causing a scandal. It made me remember the old film, "They Shoot Horses, Don't They?" (although that film wasn't about horses). But we don't permit horses who have no hope of recovering from a painful injury to survive. We act to end their suffering as soon as possible. What sense does it make not to grant the same privilege to people who are suffering from incurable conditions or simply from enduring, intractable pain?

I mean, why should such people suffer needlessly? If those of us who believe in abortion rights hold that women, not doctors and certainly not politicians, should have dominion over their own bodies, why shouldn't we have dominion over our own lives? Don't our bodies belong to us?

This same question was raised in another old film I saw some years ago, which was entitled, "Whose Life Is it, Anyway?" In the film, the main character, played by Richard Dreyfuss, is a sculptor who becomes paralyzed from the neck down as a result of an automobile accident. Since his life depends on the use of his hands (his whole life is sculpting, he avers), he finds there is no point in living, and he chooses to refuse treatment in order to die. The drama of the film centers on the reactions to his choice on the part of his friends and the medical staff and hinges on the question whether the medical and legal institutions in which he was enmeshed will respect or prevent his choice to die.

This film also brings to the fore a central thorny issue of

Englehart's book – whether dying is a matter for medicine to decide or whether it should be regarded as human right. One of the doctors who has been active for a long time in the right-to-die movement, a man named Philip Nitschke, the author of the book, *The Peaceful Pill Handbook,* is a staunch defender of the latter position. This is how he frames the issue:

> *The medical model is where we see this as a service that you provide to the sick. If a person gets sick enough, and all the doctors agree, the person who is very sick and keen to die gets lawful help to die. The rights model, which I'm strongly in favor of, says this has got nothing to do with sickness. The idea is: having a peaceful death is a human right. And as a right it's not something you have to ask permission for. In other words, it's something you have simply because you're a person of this planet. The rights model, of course, means that doctors don't necessarily have to be involved.... The right of a rational adult to a peaceful death, at the time of one's own choosing, is fundamental.*

This perspective, still very controversial and the subject of heated, often rancorous, debate, is nevertheless seemingly gaining strength and more adherents in America. After all, it's well known that the right to die movement is already strong in such countries as the Netherlands, Belgium and Switzerland, and even physician-assisted death, as limited and hedged in by complex legal and medical regulations as it is, is now permitted in a number of states. If you were to read Englehart's book – and I strongly recommend it to anyone with an interest in these matters – you would quickly learn about all the latest techniques doctors and engineers have devised to ease people into death, the books available on the subject, the organizations devoted to the right-to-die movement, and so forth.

But there is still another reason to think that in the coming years this movement will continue to grow stronger, and that has to do with demographics. The elderly are now the fastest growing segment in America. In 2010, there were about 40 million Americans 65 or older. By 2030, it is projected that one in five American will have reached that age. If so, that means we will soon be saddled with a population that is increasingly afflicted with dementia or otherwise seriously physically compromised. And since a quarter of all Medicare spending goes to people in the last year of their lives, there will be an even greater financial strain on our social networks, such as Medicare, Medicaid and Social Security.

What this portends, to put it crudely, is that in the future, many old and infirm people will be virtually begging to die, their younger relatives will be motivated to help them to do so (since their economic well-being is threatened by having so much of our national wealth having to be diverted to care for the elderly) and organizations like the AARP and other organizations that lobby for the old will have to become advocates for the right-to-die movement. You can see the writing on the wall. The demographics make it plain. We can no longer afford (literally) to let death take its course. We must find ways to ease the burdens of life on the old by helping them to die with dignity and lessen the financial burdens on the young so that they can live without themselves suffering unduly. Medical technology has indeed enabled people to live longer than ever, but it has also served to prolong their years of pain and debility, ending with their complete dependence on others. Does this make sense? Is it humane?

Before concluding this essay, there is one more issue I need to deal with that has been with us from the very beginning. It was implicit in the story I told at the outset about Virginia Hine's death and was explicitly brought out in the film I mentioned, "Whose Life Is It, Anyway?" And that is the question having to do with the S-word. Should such deaths be regarded as suicides? And if so, what can people expect to experience when they die in this way? This is a question that can be addressed, even if not definitively answered, by the research on near-death experiences for people who nearly die, but don't, as a result of a suicide attempt. In fact, whether one prefers to call deaths like Ginny's "chosen deaths," or regards them as a form of rational suicide, we still want to know what will such people experience when they cross the threshold into the house of death.

But first, let's look at some statistics concerning suicide in America, especially for the elderly. Older adults make up 12% of the US population, but account for 18% of all suicide deaths. This is an alarming statistic, as the elderly are the fastest growing segment of the population, making the issue of later-life suicide a major public health priority. Moreover, in 2018, seniors ages 85 and older had the second-highest suicide rate in the nation. From what I have already written, I think you will understand why. Finally, estimates suggest that for every reported death by suicide, an additional 29 attempts are made.

Now turning to what we know about what people experience when they make an unsuccessful suicide attempt, the data both from my research and that of my longtime friend and colleague, the psychiatrist Bruce Greyson, are in agreement. Although many people who come close to death in this way remember nothing (that is true as well for other modes of near-death onset, such as a cardiac arrest), those who do tend to report the same kind of classic, radiant NDE as do people who nearly die from injuries or cardiac conditions. Greyson has found that about 25% of his suicide cases report such NDEs. My findings were similar. I concluded therefore that there is nothing unique about NDEs triggered by a failed suicide attempt.

Furthermore, most of those who do experience an NDE are not tempted to try suicide again, and, indeed, often conclude that suicide would solve nothing – even if they had succeeded, they seem to feel that they would have to deal with the same issues that prompted their attempt in the first place. But most importantly, they typically don't feel that they would be punished, much less "sent to hell," because of trying to kill themselves. As with NDEs that occur in other ways, they are not judged, but usually experience compassionate understanding and unconditional love during the time they hover between life and death.

However, most of my cases, and I suspect this is also true for Greyson's, involve people who are relatively young and who normally have attempted suicide because of personal problems, such as alcoholism, drug addiction, financial troubles or a failed love affair. These we may call collectively "despair-based" suicide attempts. But for the elderly, the motivations tend to be different in many cases. For them, there is often a feeling that their lives are complete, that they are suffering needlessly for no good reason, and that they simply "want to go home." For such people, suicide is more of a considered rational decision, not one governed by an impulsive act stemming from an acute condition of despair and despondency. At least, this is the sense one gets from reading the many cases to be found in Englehart's book.

The trouble is, so far as I know, we don't have much if any data on what is experienced by elderly people who take this route toward death, in large part, of course, because they succeed in taking their lives. So here I can only speculate.

First, from all the research I've done on NDEs, I know that someone who nearly dies in whatever way is not judged. Instead, they tend to be greeted by a warm loving light. They feel that they are home, where they belong and where, in some eternal sense, they have always been. As one man I know well put it, "It was eternity. It's like I was always there and would always be there, and that my existence on earth was just a brief instant."

Since I've mentioned several films in this essay, I can't help thinking of a famous film actor from another era, Charles Boyer. He often played the part of a sophisticated lover. These days, he is probably best remembered for his role in "Gaslight" in which he starred with Ingrid Bergman.

I mention him here because I remember reading some years ago that he so loved his wife that when she died, he was so distraught that he could not bear to live without her. Two days after her death, he committed suicide by taking Seconal.

I was very touched when I learned that. Personally, I just cannot persuade myself that Charles Boyer, when he took that last dance into the Light, would have been made to suffer for his actions. No, that's just inconceivable to me.

Likewise for my friend, Ginny, who also chose to die so that she could again be with her beloved husband, Aldie.

It is my profound hope and prayer for all those who, having lived a full life and who no longer choose to live in pain, that they, too, will find surcease in the Light. That would only be just, don't you think?

The Silent Epidemic of Our Times

I recently read a very touching story about a woman named Virginia, who is 92 years old, and her cat, Jennie. She adores her cat who is almost always nearby. She likes to look at Jennie's green eyes. She likes that Jennie is with her in the morning when Virginia wakes up. And sometimes when Virginia feels sad, she just sits in her soft armchair while Jennie rests on Virginia's stomach. She nuzzles, purrs, stretches and just does her cat-like things.

Talking to an interviewer, Virginia said, "I can't believe that this has meant as much as it has to me." When she dies, she thought she might bring Jennie with her.

Jennie is a robot.

I came across this vignette in a recent article in The New Yorker that was written by Katie Englehart, the author of the book, *The Inevitable*, which I featured in a previous essay. In the article, she was addressing a problem that two English researchers, writing in *The Lancet*, had characterized in the following way:

Imagine a condition that makes a person irritable, depressed, and self-centered, and is associated with a 26% increase in the risk of premature mortality. Imagine too that in industrialised countries around a third of people are affected by this condition, with one person in 12 affected severely, and that these proportions are increasing. Income, education, sex, and ethnicity are not protective, and the condition is contagious. The effects of the condition are not attributable to some peculiarity of the character of a subset of individuals, they are a result of the condition affecting ordinary people.

The condition to which these authors are referring, as you might have guessed, is loneliness. And, as we also now know, this condition is particularly acute among the elderly, which is why caregivers have been interested to see whether providing them with robot pets will help to alleviate their loneliness. In fact, as a number of researchers and scholars have recently pointed out, the pervasiveness of loneliness among the old in America has now reached what the Surgeon General, Vivek Murthy, was frank to call an "epidemic." But in contrast to the pandemic we have all been through for the last year and half, this has mostly been a silent epidemic. The plight of the elderly, despite suffering unduly from the pandemic and dying in much greater numbers than younger people, did not receive the kind of sustained attention that we gave to families having to cope with children underfoot or workers who had lost their jobs.

This is understandable, of course. As a society, we no longer venerate the old, assuming we once did; all too often, we simply abandon, forget or ignore them. To be sure, individual family members usually continue to care for their elderly loved ones when they can. And we have all heard horrific stories of the contagion of COVID and resultant deaths that plagued our nursing and other old age homes during the first year of the pandemic. But *as a society,* we no longer provide the kind of social welfare net that permits most older people to continue to live out their lives in relative comfort in the company of other family members.

There was a time, of course, when, even in America, many people lived in extended families, either in the same house or nearby in the same neighborhood. In those days, when grandma became old and frail and could no longer hear well, she would still be cared for, and could still enjoy the loving company of her family. These days, however, grandma is usually shipped off to a nursing home to live among decrepit and often demented strangers, who cry out piteously during the night and during the day often sit, vacantly, strapped into their wheelchairs. This happened to my mother, too, when she had become old (I was living in Connecticut then while she, who had never flown, had to remain in California). During those years, I would continue to visit her as often as I could arrange to come out to California, but every time I had to leave her in her bed alone and without friends or other family, I felt a wracking guilt.

But even when older people can continue to live in their own homes, they are often left alone, and when that happens, they can suffer from acute loneliness and feelings of abandonment. And more and more of our elderly *do* live alone now – more than ever – as a result of the modern way of family life which has seen the rise of isolated nuclear family settings at the expense of extended family networks. Statistics show that nowadays almost 30% of Americans over the age of 65 live by themselves, most of them women. And during the period when COVID raged, this isolation, as we all know, was even more of a torment to the old and to their families who could no longer see and comfort them. How many of these elderly people died, alone and afraid, without a hand to hold? One can only shudder when one imagines people dying in this way. How many tears have been shed by their helpless family members? Perhaps you were such a person or knew others who had to endure such emotional and traumatic distress.

Even before COVID struck, however, the deleterious effects of isolation among the old were evident to researchers. Let me take just a moment to acquaint you with the range and severity of some of these effects.

To begin with, 43% of the elderly in America complain about being lonely. According to Englehart, loneliness can "prompt a heightened inflammatory response, which can increase a person's risk for a vast range of pathologies, including dementia, depression, high blood pressure, and stroke." To amplify this point, consider the following statistics that come from a book dealing with the effects of social isolation in older adults:

- Social isolation has been associated with a significantly increased risk of premature mortality from all causes.

- Social isolation has been associated with an approximately 50 percent increased risk of developing dementia.

- Loneliness among heart failure patients has been associated with a nearly four times increased risk of death, 68 percent increased risk of hospitalization, and 57 percent increased risk of emergency department visits.

- Poor social relationships (characterized by social isolation or loneliness) have been associated with a 29 percent increased risk of incident coronary heart disease and a 32 percent increased risk of stroke.

Of course, old age in itself is hard enough to endure for most of us oldsters, quite apart from the dangers, physical and emotional, of isolation, which I have just briefly adumbrated. The so-called "golden years" are really just the olden years when sentiment is absent and the reality of life as one ages is bereft of any illusory euphemism. Growing old is scary enough when one contemplates the prospect and then the reality of increasing decrepitude, loneliness, illness and then, finally, dying and death. If you have the misfortunate of living long enough, you may even find yourself not only alone but without anyone any longer knowing you who are and what you have been in your life. This is probably the most terrifying kind of existential isolation.

I remember when I was in my early eighties and was writing some (mostly) humorous essays about my own vicissitudes of aging that I eventually collected into a little book I puckishly called *Waiting to Die,* I had one of those moments of anticipatory existential fright. This is what I wrote at the time:

One day long ago I had a shocking realization. I received a new credit card whose expiration date was November, 2023, when I would be almost 88 years old. Surely, I thought, I would expire long before that. But, then, a horrible thought occurred to me: What if I don't?! What if I live to 88?

Honestly, before seeing that card, I had never imagined such a thing. No, no! Will I still be walking on this road toward death, still waiting to die, for years to come? What a ghastly thought.

I realized I'm not afraid to die; I'm now afraid of living too long!

At that time, I could still half-joke about such a prospect, but now that I am already 87, it seems that some of my fears may no longer be a laughing matter!

A few years ago, the well-known physician, Ezekiel Emmanuel (you have probably seen him often interviewed on television where he became a frequent commentator on the pandemic), wrote a now famous piece in The Atlantic, which he provocatively entitled, "Why I Hope to Die at 75." In it, he reflected my own thinking, but took the time to lay out his reasons. This is how his article began:

That's how long I want to live: 75 years.

This preference drives my daughters crazy. It drives my brothers crazy. My loving friends think I am crazy. They think that I can't mean what I say; that I haven't thought clearly about this, because there is so much in the world to see and do. To convince me of my errors, they enumerate the myriad people I know who are over 75 and doing quite well. They are certain that as I get closer to 75, I will push the desired age back to 80, then 85, maybe even 90.

I am sure of my position. Doubtless, death is a loss. It deprives us of experiences and milestones, of time spent with our spouse and children. In short, it deprives us of all the things we value.

But here is a simple truth that many of us seem to resist: living too long is also a loss. It renders many of us, if not disabled, then faltering and declining, a state that may not be worse than death but is nonetheless deprived. It robs us of our creativity and ability to contribute to work, society, the world. It transforms how people experience us, relate to us, and, most important, remember us. We are no longer remembered as vibrant and engaged but as feeble, ineffectual, even pathetic.

Exactly. Which is why I argued in my previous essay that people should have the right to terminate their own lives. Emmanuel would not choose to do that, but many people who no longer wish to live doubtless would if they could do so peacefully. Who, when young, dreams of getting old? Instead, we pretend it won't happen to us. I never really thought it would happen to me either. But one day, after I had turned 81, I realized that my time had come.

Right now, even though I live alone (and have for many years – it's easier for us introverts), I am lucky to have a loving girlfriend, now nearly 81 herself, who is able to spend some time with me as well as a caretaker who can assist me when I need someone to go grocery shopping or do errands for me. But my three children all live far from me, and I would never want to burden them with my care if one day I should find myself alone in this world. But who knows – it may be that I will eventually be one of those people I have been writing about – on my own, sick and feeling forlorn, lost in my dotage, just waiting to die. Knowing what I have learned about the effects of isolation, I am not keen on spending my last days like this, even if I should have a robot cat to keep me company.

Of course, old age needn't be a drag or a seemingly unending series of tribulations and sorrows. It's important to keep things in balance after all. As Emmanuel implies, old age can also be rewarding and full of pleasures, including sex. I have an old girlfriend, now well into her 80s, who frequently writes me about her deeply satisfying sex life with her husband. And there are certainly people in their nineties who are happy still to be alive and able to enjoy life.

Since this essay has been grim and uncharacteristically sober (at least for me), suppose we take a moment for a little levity to lighten the mood. One thing that I've been struck by is how many comics live to a great age and seem to leave this world laughing, at least figuratively speaking. To take one example, I can choose one of my favorite comics from an earlier era, George Burns, whom you may remember as God since late in life he became famous (again) for playing God in a film with John Denver. I mention him and comics generally because, as I have previously argued in some of my blogs, humor is often the best defense against the trials of aging and the prospect of death.

George Burns died at 100, and like other centenarians, he was asked to explain the secret of his longevity. He was inclined to attribute his success to smoking cigars daily. But there were other factors as well that contributed to his aging well until the end, as witness this obituary:

George Burns died at age 100 on March 9, 1996. Mr. Burns spent his lifetime in show business and created millions of laughs. It is reported that Mr. Burns was buried with three cigars in his pocket, had on his toupee, his ring and watch, which was a gift from his wife, and in the pocket of his suit were "his keys and his wallet with ten 100-dollar bills, a five, and three ones, so wherever he went to play bridge he'd have enough money."

Several years ago, he was asked by an interviewer if he ever considered retiring. "Retire to what?" an amused Mr. Burns asked. "I play bridge for two hours a day to get away from work. Why the hell would I want to retire to play bridge 24 hours a day?" George Burns played bridge every day of his life. He loved bridge. But at 3 o'clock, he could be in the middle of a hand, he'd stand up (and say) "Thank you gentlemen," and go home to take a nap. He used to say: "Bridge is a game that separates the men from the boys. It also separates husbands and wives."

Burns was perhaps one of the best bridge players in Hollywood. Well, if not the best, the funniest.

I loved George Burns, and his raspy voice – from all those cigars, no doubt. He knew how to enjoy himself and when to rest. He also did yoga. We oldsters can all take a lesson from George Burns. Keep laughing and don't allow yourself to languish – that's the ticket.

Still, George was the rare exception. Most people suffer when they get very old and often yearn to be free of the burden of living. Nevertheless, even though life is hard for the old and is in end universally fatal, as long as we are still here, we old-timers have to make the best of it. What will help us get through our battles with loneliness if robotic animals aren't enough?

We are social creatures, and older people, who were so cruelly deprived of that kind of vital contact during the pandemic, are particularly vulnerable to the lack of face-to-face interaction. They can starve psychologically without it, but they can rebound and even thrive again with it. We must find ways to address the social deficit of the aged in order to forestall, if not completely defeat, the insidious dangers of loneliness.

And social workers and other caregivers have not been slow to realize this. Here's just one example of this kind of intervention:

The good news is that friendships reduce the risk of mortality or developing certain diseases and can speed recovery in those who fall ill. Moreover, simply reaching out to lonely people can jump-start the process of getting them to engage with neighbors and peers, according to Robin Caruso of CareMore Health, which operates in 8 states and the District of Columbia with a focus on Medicare patients. Her "Togetherness" initiative aims to combat "an epidemic of loneliness" among seniors through weekly phone calls, home visits and community programs.

What can *you* do? It's obvious: Visit the old. So what if they just natter and chatter – they matter! Now that the COVID cloud is perhaps finally beginning to lift, don't go out solely for your own pleasure. Do you have a loved one or someone you know who is living alone or in a nursing home? If so, visit them. Even better, bring them a pet, a real pet, not a robot, if they don't have one. And don't just visit once. Come back. Help to assuage their loneliness. You'll be doing a mitzvah. You will be old one day yourself. Sew some good karma while you can. It will come back to you.

Englehart found that many older people whom she visited were reluctant to see her leave. They relished the time with her; they wanted her to come back. As she writes about Virginia:

> It was the same with almost every robot owner I met. "I haven't had anybody to talk to for a while, so chatter, chatter, chatter," Virginia said, when I first called. Near the end of my visit to her home, she insisted that I take a doughnut for the road and told me to come back sometime. She thought she would probably be around, though she also wondered if she would die in the big empty house: "Maybe this is the year."
>
> "Your bags are packed, right?" her daughter-in-law said, laughing.
>
> "Gotta go sometime," Virginia said. When she died, she thought she might bring Jennie with her. She liked the idea of being buried with the cat in her arms.

Being Mortal While Being Immortal

If you read books or listen to podcasts on spirituality, you are bound to be told – many times *ad infinitum* – that "we are spiritual beings having a human experience." I usually wince with dismay when I hear such twaddle repeated over and over. Not that it's in the category of a Trumpian "big lie," which is obviously a big lie in its own wrong; I actually believe that I am an eternal being who has dipped into the illusion of time in order to learn certain lessons, such as being able to tie one's shoelaces without assistance, until I can be sprung from this temporal prison. It's just that I have a pedant's revulsion whenever I encounter such pap. It's the same category as another spiritual bromide, such as "there are no accidents." You've heard that one, too, right? To which I am wont to counter, "except for chance events, errors, mistakes and random mayhem." Yes, I admit it: I am an unrepentant curmudgeon when it comes to spiritual clichés.

However much such spiritual drivel may arouse my spleen, I have always been a sucker for a good quip or a witty zinger. One of my favorite characters who is as quick with a quip as anyone I know is my fellow curmudgeon, Woody Allen. Yes, I know his reputation has been tarnished in recent years from all the to-do about whether he did or didn't, but I have always been partial to Woody, not only for his mordant wit, but perhaps because we are virtual contemporaries, he having arrived on the planet just twelve days ahead of me, in 1935. You will see where I am going with this shortly, but for now "here are some of my favorite things" that Woody has uttered to amuse us:

Nature and I are two.

Man can't live on bread alone; he also needs a beverage.

I don't believe in the afterlife, although I am bringing a change in underwear.

But what will be of more interest to us in what follows is suggested by some of Woody's quips about death. For instance:

I am not afraid of death, I just don't want to be there when it happens.

There are worse things in life than death. Have you ever spent an evening with an insurance salesman?

I don't want to achieve immortality through my work. I want to achieve it through not dying.

Clearly, Woody is not keen on death. He says that he is firmly "against it." Most people would doubtless agree and would rather not think about it. If you are under sixty, you probably would rather think about other things, such as sex. In which case, you might not want to bother reading the rest of this essay.

But we are actually not going to talk about death so much as what happens when you get old and have to face *the prospect of death.* This is when your telomeres begin to shorten, when you start developing tumors or cancer or heart disease, when your body has begun to betray you and you live in fear and chronic, often severe, pain. In other words, we are talking about your future, and mine. We are talking about the disease from which none of us will recover – aging.

I'm afraid this will be rather grim reading – until the end. And there won't be much more humor to leaven the load. But there will still be the occasional zinger, as in this famous remark of Bette Davis: "Old age is no place for sissies." If you live long enough, though, you will be living in that place. Let's check it out before we get there.

Our guide will be the gifted writer and physician, Atul Gawande, the author of the best-seller of a few years back, *Being Mortal*. In what follows, I will be drawing on his very readable and enlightening book about what's it's like to be facing death in America at this time. What he has to tell us won't reassure Woody, but it will help us be better prepared for the inevitable.

For years I resisted reading this book, despite its excellent reviews and the urging of my cousin, Cliff, a retired cardiologist, who assured me it was a "terrific" book. But having spent forty years consorting with the once nearly dead who had reported their NDEs to me, I figured I had already devoted enough of my life thinking and writing about death. But, truth to tell, I was just like everyone else when it came to thinking about dying itself. Frankly, I would rather not – die. Or even think about what my later years might entail if I ever should find myself heading toward that final abyss. After all, despite my infirmities and decrepitude, I was actually in pretty good health. I had never had a serious disease; I was still enjoying life and had continued to write and keep as active mentally as I could. I had been extremely lucky, especially compared to many of my friends who were far worse off than I was or who had already kicked the bucket. What me, worry?

But like many elderly people nowadays, I live alone, and as I am now heading toward 87, I had to admit that I could no longer pretend that I was invulnerable to what are often loosely and playfully called "the ravages of age." After all, no male member of my immediate family had ever lived to 87. How long could I really expect my good luck streak to continue? Most oldsters like to think they will die peacefully in their sleep after a happy life. But, face it, that is as rare as winning the lottery, a delusional wish-fulfillment.

You may not die like Tolstoy's fictional character, Ivan Illich, by screaming in agony for three days before your death, but if you were to read Gawande's book of horrors, you would quickly learn that you are not likely to enjoy your descent toward death once your body begins to fall apart, as it will.

So, in the end, I figuratively girded my loins, and delved into Gawande's book. In fact, I was already familiar with Gawande. I'd been reading his work for years, mostly in *The New Yorker*, for which he's long been a staff writer. But as a writer and medical scholar, he has had a very distinguished career. He has been awarded many literary prizes, is a MacArthur Fellow, and is on the faculty of Harvard. He is widely and deservedly recognized as one of the most outstanding writer/physicians in America. So I knew I would learn a lot from this man.

Still, he begins his book for covering a lot of the ground I have discussed in some of my previous essays. For example, although Gawande grew up in America, he refers to his Indian background where typically older people are revered and remain in their families until their death. His parental grandfather, for example, lived until almost the age of 110, and only died because of a freak accident.

In cultures with traditional extended family structures, old people are not warehoused into nursing homes as they tend to be in our modern culture. But with the rise of isolated nuclear families in our own time, many old people are effectively deposited into nursing homes where strangers care for them and family members may visit only occasionally, if at all. Or, since increasingly, old people, especially women, live by themselves, they may become ill, which creates still other problems. One way or another, the situation of old people can often be fraught with risk or even greater peril – complete abandonment.

But here's what makes it worse, as Gawande points out. In former times, people didn't live to a great age. During ancient Roman times, for example, the average life expectancy was about thirty years. Even in the Middle Ages, it was rare to live beyond one's fifties. And when people did die, they tended to die quickly. Even in George Washington's time, dying could come overnight, as it did for him. On December 13th, 1799, he suddenly became ill. By the next night, he was gone.

Being interested in classical music, I can't help thinking of all those famous composers that never made it out of their thirties. Schubert, for instance, died at 31, and Mozart, Mendelssohn, Chopin, Carl Maria von Weber, and Henry Purcell never lived to see forty.

But now, thanks to advances in sanitation, diet, and medical technology, people can live to very advanced ages, which means that, relatively suddenly, our country and most others in the developed world, are struggling to support vast numbers of older people who can no longer live independently. Enormous amounts of money have to be expended, especially in the last year of elderly people's lives, to house and take care of them. They become, as sociologists put it, "surplus populations."

And since most families can no longer take care of their own, institutions arise to warehouse the old until they die. Thus, we have seen the rise, especially since the middle of the last century, of the obscenity of nursing homes.

Of course, there are many caring people who work in such places, but these are poorly paid jobs, and for many, it is "just a job." How many of us dream that one day we will wind up in such a dismal and depressing setting, being taken care of by a succession of strangers, when we have lost all agency over our own fate? But this could indeed be your fate one day, my friends. This is how your life could end when you are sick, infirm and perhaps demented. It could happen to me, too, of course, but I would be tempted to say, "over my dead body!" Truly, I would rather die than to end up in such a place, wouldn't you?

Gawande spends a lot of time talking about life in nursing homes, and offers a number of case histories of people who were forced to live out the end of their lives there. They make for frightening reading. And, remember, Gawande was visiting such places and writing about them before COVID hit. We all remember in the beginning of the pandemic that nursing homes were often settings where COVID could easily spread, causing many people to die, perhaps a blessing in a way, though dying of COVID, alone and without family, had to be a ghastly way to expire.

Have you ever visited such "homes?" I have. During the last years of my mother's life when I was still teaching at the University of Connecticut, I had to place my mother, then in her early 80s, in such a home in Berkeley. I would visit her as often as I could, and once I was able to move back to California, I was able to visit almost weekly until she died.

I am an only child from a very small family, and in all the years she lived there – she died when she was nearly 89 – no one else ever visited her. (Sometimes, however, my girlfriend at the time, would accompany me.) What you would have seen if you had been with me is fairly typical of such homes. You enter and you see a long corridor of people strapped into their wheelchairs, drooling or cursing of just sitting there, mute and absent. Many are demented, of course. My mother shared a room with a succession of women she didn't know, some of whom would rave during the night, she told me.

My mother was beginning to lose her hearing, but she was still, until the near the end, mentally competent. She could no longer walk, so on nice days I would push her wheelchair around the neighborhood (fortunately, the streets were flat), or take her out in back and read to her (she liked to listen to short stories by Chekhov) or play gin rummy with her. But she couldn't read, didn't want to listen to the radio or watch TV. She didn't even like to be touched. She mostly remained quiet and just stayed in her bed. She had no life. The place had no life. My mother wasn't mistreated. The staff, so far as I could tell, were kind and caring people. But, still, I felt absolutely dreadful every time I had to leave, seeing her there in her bed, lying passively, not even able to say or wave goodbye. I would kiss her on her forehead and say I would see her again next time until there was no next time.

Gawande, who in preparation for writing his book, spent a great deal of time in places like those in which my mother vegetated and died, came away with the direct knowledge of how much such institutions fail to serve the needs of the people in their care. At the outset of his book, he offers an almost savage indictment of the failures of modern medicine:

> *You don't have to spend much time with the elderly or those with terminal illness to see how often medicine fails the people it is supposed to help. The waning days of our lives are given over to treatments that addle our brains and sap our bodies for a sliver's chance of benefit. They are spent in institutions – nursing homes and intensive care units – where regimented, anonymous routines cut us off from all the things that matter to us in life. Our reluctance to honestly examine the experience of aging and dying has increased the harm we inflict on people and denied them the most basic comforts they need most. Lacking a coherent view of how people might live successfully all the way to the very end, we have allowed our fates to be controlled by the imperatives of medicine, technology, and strangers.*

But in his travels, Gawande didn't just wander through the often soulless and depressing interiors of nursing homes; he also spent a lot of time seeking out experts in the field of death and dying, such as elderly geriatricians (apparently themselves a dying breed), but especially innovators who were trying to change the culture of such institutions so that they would become much more than warehouses for people who were suffering and merely marking time, as my mother did, waiting for the end to come.

Many of these pioneers had come up with ingenious solutions to enliven the daily lives of the residents of these homes, and the stories Gawande recounts in his book are very inspiring and hopeful – and often hilarious. I only have space to relate one such story, but it shows what is possible if one has imagination, pluck and perseverance.

In upstate New York in 1991, a young Harvard-trained physician named Bill Thomas became the director of a nursing home. He didn't like what he saw there, and had an idea. He wanted to attack what he termed the three plagues of nursing home life: boredom, loneliness and helplessness. So to bring some life into this nursing home, he proposed to bring dogs and cats – and a hundred parakeets into this facility!

The administrators thought he was nuts. Besides, this would never fly. There was no way they could get such a wacky plan approved, much less funded. But Bill Thomas was the kind of guy who would not be denied. He proved to be incredibly dynamic and persuasive. And in the end, he was able to do everything he had in mind.

Once the animals came into the home, there was of course pandemonium and confusion, but ultimately most of the residents were delighted. The animals were a big hit and the residents' spirits were uplifted. Many were brought out of their shells of isolation, as Gawande relates:

> *"People who we had believed weren't able to speak started speaking," Thomas said. People who had been completely withdrawn and nonambulatory started coming to the nurses' station saying, 'I'll take the dog for a walk.'" All the parakeets were adopted and named by the residents. The lights turned back on in people's eyes.*

Researchers studied the effect of this program for two years. The findings? The number or prescriptions were half that of conventional nursing homes. The need for psychotropic drugs, like Haldol, decreased. Total drug costs fell 38%, compared to other similar homes. Deaths fell 15%. In short, Thomas's plan was an improbable but undeniable success.

Gawande's book, though it is full of heartrending stories of people's ultimately futile battles with their illnesses – and the reader gets to know many of these people, as Gawande makes sure to stay in touch with them – but it is also studded with stories like that of Bill Thomas, of people who buck the system and find ways to bring hope and compassionate care into the lives of those who would otherwise be forgotten and left to suffer.

Suffering is inevitable, of course, especially for the old and infirm and those afflicted by incurable illnesses, but ways *are* being found to mitigate that suffering by paying compassionate attention to the special needs and goals of people who find themselves, as many of us will one day, dealing with intractable illnesses as they approach and often yearn for death.

Gawande himself, as gifted as a surgeon as he is, is very forthright about his own shortcomings as a physician when it comes to learning how to be with the dying. Doctors, after all, are not trained to deal with the dying; they often don't know how to talk to or be with such people, and sometimes lose interest in them when they feel they can no longer help them. Doctors are taught to fix things, but you can't fix death. If you regard death as the enemy, then the enemy always wins in the end. It's understandable that many doctors would prefer to ignore or slight the dying in order to attend to the living.

But Gawande in the course of doing his research for his book and talking to so many people has come to learn a lot about how to be with the dying, and he has advice for his fellow doctors, which he sums up in three questions they should be sure to put to such people:

What are your biggest fears and concerns?
What goals are most important to you?
What tradeoffs ae you willing to make, and what ones are unacceptable to you?

Gawande cites research that shows one of the most important

things that doctors can do for the dying is to engage them in discussions about such issues, and not just the treatments that they could perform, which ultimately often prove useless and just extend their suffering. "Doctors everywhere," Gawande writes, "become all too ready to offer false hopes, leading families to empty bank accounts ... and take money from their children's education for futile treatments."

The dying don't just want technical information, which often just confuses them, anyway. How do they know what's best for them? No, they want doctors to listen to them, to their fears, to understand their goals, to engage with them, and not just to offer their "expert opinions." In short, doctors need to learn to shut up at such times and listen. That can make all the difference.

As Gawande eloquently concludes:

> *Our most cruel failure in how we treat the sick and the aged is the failure to recognize that they have priorities beyond merely being safe and living longer; that the chance to shape one's story is essential to sustaining meaning in life; that we have the opportunity to refashion our institutions, our culture, and our conversation in ways that transform the possibilities for the last chapters of everyone's lives.*

Gawande is the son of two physicians, and his father was a distinguished urologist, a man of immense energy, as healthy as "a Brahma bull," Gawande says, but in his seventies, he finally begins to learn that he, too, will have to face his mortality. Always healthy, he becomes sick and then gravely ill. The last pages of this incredibly moving book become even more poignant when Gawande has to deal with his own father's illness and, ultimately, with his death. I found this part of the book very tender, sad, and so aptly fitting, as if everything that Gawande had learned in conducting the research for his book, could at the end be distilled as his final gift to his beloved father. What a beautiful tribute to a loving father from a loving son.

A Personal Postscript

Gawande does not seem to be a religious man. I gather that like most physicians he has a secular outlook on life. His concern throughout the book is of course on questions of mortality, and not with what may come afterward. But I, who have mostly been concerned in my work with what happens *at* the point of death and with what people realize at that liminal transcendent moment, have a different point of view. What struck me in reading this book is how desperately people cling to life, and how, even when they long to die, their families often urge their doctors "to do everything possible" to preserve their lives of their loved ones, even if that only serves to prolong their agony.

In one of my previous essays, I recounted the case of the world-famous psychiatrist, Irving Yalom, who resisted to the last his wife's desperate pleas to be allowed to die because of unremitting pain from terminal cancer. She wanted death, but her husband didn't want her to leave – to leave him.

I wish people could know that when facing death, despite the pain, there is no reason to fear. I suppose I am guilty of resorting to a cliché of my own when I say that through my work, I have learned that "death is not a dead end." Maybe I should write a book called "Being Immortal." For I really do believe that we *are* eternal beings, and that we are all destined to return to our true home once our life on this plane ends. Maybe this, too, is something that those who attend the dying might want to keep in mind. After all, anything that could ease the fears of the dying may also serve to reassure those about to make their final passage to whatever may lie beyond this mortal life of ours.

In Memoriam:
The Last Days of Bonnie Treadwell

October 28, 2022
Bonnie Writes:

Dear Ken — I am pasting in below a letter I recently wrote to an Arizona friend …

"I'm wearing my beloved grandmother's wedding ring now … I called/call her Mammy, my true mother …. because I'm begging her for help. I have some things to tell you. Since about the first part of August, my physical body has gone downhill really quick. Just almost overnight. First, I couldn't lift my leg to get in the tub/shower. Was puzzled … why can't I lift my legs? … and from there things just got worse. Then I couldn't get into bed, couldn't get in the car, legs just not working.

To back up a little and probably tell you things I've already told you … I was born with lipedema which morphs into lymphedema as age progresses, causing varicose veins, ruined knees, major swelling, etc. (Such fun.) I also was born with scoliosis, and other back problems then came along for the ride, one of which is spinal stenosis. Now that's a real fun one … prevents walking, a biggie. Other

129

major things happen as you get older because spinal nerves are being impacted.

Truth is, I've lived way too long. I really thought I would be outta here before those nerves got into a tangle. Never thought I'd live to almost 90. Now I've got to deal with it. There's more … I can't breathe … was just diagnosed with pulmonary fibrosis and pulmonary hypertension. Oh, and that's not all … add congestive heart failure to that, and even more attacks from lymphedema on now my whole body, torso, arms, more on already deformed legs, and, oh my tummy looks like I'm overdue pregnant with quads. All of this swelling makes the skin very tight and painful.

This body is worn out … I hurt almost everywhere … and, frankly I don't want to be saved and will NOT go to a hospital. I always wondered what would take me out, and now I guess I know, but it's so many I don't know which one will do the deed! Was hoping for a quick heart attack … or slipping away in my sleep somehow.

That said, I'm ready to go and am begging my beloved grandmother, my Mammy, to please come and get me. That probably won't work, so don't get out your crying handkerchief just yet. If I'd been smart, I would have somehow gotten something long ago to take to stash away until I wanted it, but just couldn't imagine living this long.

My strong determination to hang around until the pandemic was over and until Brenda has a somewhat normal life again has wilted. The desire to not leave her here by herself in this house with no one but Bootsie … her dog … has kept me motivated to stay. (I had 2 years of almost complete isolation while living in Kermit, and nearly went nuts and don't want her to experience that.)

But I have now wimped out. And what lies ahead is not easy to think about. I don't want to put Brenda through my care-taking which is going to be intense if I keep on living forever and ever. Already she's remodeled the bathroom for me, and I probably won't be around long to use it that much ... I hope. *Have I told you that Brenda is an angel?*

Just thought you might want to know all of this but there's no need to fret ... unfortunately, I'll probably live long enough to spend lots of time regretting even more my multitudes of mistakes and errors throughout this too-long lifetime! ---

PS ... My grandmother's wedding ring is a gold buckle ring, Victorian/Edwardian style ... they married in 1909. One time she lost it in the garden and found it a year later ... in the garden! I love wearing it, and hope that it calls her to me ... soon."

So, here I am, Ken, telling you that I'm on hospice now and so grateful for their assistance and care. Hospice now doesn't mean what it used to mean. Mostly it's about comfort, right to the end. And the end can't come soon enough ... As you probably remember, I'm ready, just so ready, to leave this worn-out body.

Since I wrote that pasted letter (above) to my Arizona friend, things have gone downhill even more. Am now on oxygen, 24/7, and breathing is a real problem, even with oxygen. Sometimes I'd like to cry, but it takes too much breath to cry!

My legs have gone numb up to my hips, although I can still walk with a walker ... more like hobbling ... but can't even begin to get in bed by myself ... Sandra has to lift my legs into bed. So embarrassing.

The hospice team checks on me and are guided by my doctor. Hospice provides most of whatever I need for comfort. Yes, morphine. And I take it gladly. I'm now a druggie ... would you believe?!?!! ☺ There'll be no hospital, no "saving." All of my paperwork is in order, right down to ordering my urn from Amazon!!

Thankfully both of my children are supportive and totally

understand that I'm ready to leave, and they don't want to see me suffer. We've had talks about it, and even some laughter, and I am so fortunate to have them. My son lives far away, so I don't see him daily like I do Sandra … who is stuck with me and has been wonderful.

Ken, I do have a great fear, though, and that is that I just keep on living, going more downhill every day … oh, gosh, I've just got to get outta here, so if you have any "pull" with anyone in the "wherever" … please use it to help me leave!!!! I'm so disappointed every morning when I wake up and I'm still here.

From reading your most recent essay, I am so pleased to see that you are handling this old age thing with cheerfulness and nary a drop of sadness and that you still enjoy the small niceties of life. That makes me happy. No one should have to deal with the roughness of my end-of-life time. So, please keep writing those essays … we old ones … those of us who are still tottering around on this woeful planet … need your cheer!

Maybe I'll beat you to that "wherever" place? If so, let's have a nice chit-chat when you arrive. However, it's been so long since I've heard from you … maybe you are already there? (And wrote your essay ahead of time?)

Because he doesn't want to say the words "goodbye", my son came up with this goodbye line for whenever he visits and leaves to go home … so I'll use it here ….

See you next time! …Love, Bonnie ♥

And, ha ha, if you answer this, I'll probably still be here ... unfortunately … and you'll get a reply if I am!

October 29, 2022
Ken replies:

Oh, gosh, Bonnie — what dreadful news!

Actually, before hearing from you, I had been planning to write to you, not just to find out how you were doing, but also to ask you for your advice since I've been having increased difficulty in walking and exercising lately. My legs feel like dead weight now. But when I read your lachrymose letter, I forgot all about my own problems.

Your situation and physical state sound so wretched, I want to weep. Nobody should have to bear this kind of torture. Old age is not just cruel; it is an obscenity.

At least you're now under hospice care, and that's clearly helping you some, but only death will cure you. Maybe you could ask one of your hospice volunteers if they could score some Fentanyl for you or something else to take you out. Or jack up your morphine. Otherwise, you just have to pray that your Mammy will come to your aid soon. If you begin to see her or other deceased relatives, it will be a sign that they are waiting to welcome you home. I pray that it will be soon. Your letter was almost unbearable to read, but it is obviously incalculably worse to be experiencing all the hardships with your body that have no cure but surcease.

At least you are blessed to have Brenda there, but I know this must be hard on her, too, and I know how much you didn't want to leave her before the pandemic subsided. But you are subsiding first and you need to go. I will pray for your release, Bonnie. I wish I had some connections with the boys upstairs, but I will do what I can to help you get home before too much more time passes.

Once you do, I will probably be along before too much more time passes. Save a seat for me.

In the meantime, Bonnie, which I hope won't be long, do you want to stay in touch, even briefly? If so, I will hold your hand, at least virtually, until you go. I will always reply as soon as I can, so please write when you can, if it helps you in any way. For now, you have all my love, dear Bonnie, and my prayers that you will soon be spared further suffering. A much better, brighter and loving world awaits you.

Love and courage

October 30, 2022
Bonnie:

Thank you for your lovely compassionate letter … it brightened my spirit, such as it is. And, yes, am still here. You're absolutely right … old age is an obscenity.

First, as to your question about your legs feeling like dead weight now, I regret to have to tell you that this is normal for spinal stenosis. The spinal nerves get all tangled up in old age (!) and the legs are affected. In my case, it got worse almost overnight. Hopefully, yours will follow the normal progression of most cases … slow progression with the possibility of slowing it down with physical therapy.

But it's too late for me. You do have some choices, though, and perhaps you need to decide if you're going to try options … which could be painful … or say "to heck with it" and just let it do what it must. For me, I decided that I'd let it progress because I'd already had too many failed surgeries and other treatments including some of the newer alternative things.

Was hoping that I'd die before it got too bad … and so here I am. Didn't die. And it's bad.

It may not turn this bad for you, Ken, because you don't have the genetic conditions that I have and that are just piling on, making it worse.

Sadly, the hospice folks and/or Brenda would get in major trouble if they over-dosed me. We do have the morphine here, and Brenda keeps records when she gives it to me. Am sure it's not worth jail-time to put me out of misery. We're much kinder to our beloved pets, aren't we?

I've not "seen" Mammy or anyone that could help me, and, believe me, I'M LOOKING. My massage therapist, who is also a death doula, has been visiting me … just for talk and comfort, and that has been a good thing … although I get very tired. Am exhausted most of the time … just walking to my room wears me out.

To answer your query, yes, please, let's keep in touch and please hold my virtual hand … and so much gratitude for doing what you can to get me outta here!

(Will save you a seat!)

October 30, 2022
Ken:

Dear Bonnie,

Before turning to you, I am sorry to tell you that I've had just a wretched day myself. Not so much with my spinal stenosis, but for days I've had bad shits and today was even worse with diarrhea, too. I've had this problem, on and off, for about two months, and it is really wearying and worrisome. I will have to try to get some medical help with it ASAP. So I'm not at my best tonight, alas, but still much better off than you are, dear Bonnie.

I know that Brenda can't really give you enough morphine to take you out without risking her own situation. I just wish the hospice people could do it. In some of the essays I've written about the Right to Die Movement, I've read of a t-shirt that says, "I want to die like a dog." Indeed, we treat our pets compassionately when there's no hope for them and when they are only suffering. Why we don't do this for human beings is a disgrace and is itself an obscenity. I just hate the thought of your having to drag yourself through your days waiting for the days to end. I just hope that you don't have many more days to wait, dear Bonnie.

Thanks for trying help me with my spinal stenosis, but PT hasn't helped me. Today, despite how lousy I felt, I was able, with difficulty, to walk partway down my block and back, but then could do 20 minutes on my bike, which surprised me. But I haven't been able to do that every day. Some days, I just can't do squat. I also find that I run out of breath doing routing household chores.

But I don't want to wimpier about my own situation when yours is so desperate. Where is your Mamma when you need her? I hope she's waiting in the wings for her cue.

But mindful of your request, I banged out an essay this morning before I started to feel too bad. I expect it will be posted later this week, perhaps on Thursday. I actually hope you won't still be here to read it.

Don't worry about me, Bonnie. Even when I am having my own troubles, I'll still be here to hold your hand, virtually, and otherwise keep you company until you are released from your body's bondage. I will continue to pray for you, too.

November 1, 2022
Bonnie:

Dear Ken — I do hope that you're feeling better by today? The ****** are not fun, and take the zip out of life, such as it is. (Morphine can mess you up, too, but the opposite.) That T-shirt you told me about is great … I totally agree!

Thisisaquicknote(maybe)becauseIthinkI'mjustgoingtocrawl back into bed in a little bit. Not breathing properly makes me feel so weak and there's a "I don't know what to do with myself" kind of thing.

Have read most of the disgusting news on my computer just now. Have stopped watching TV because it's so difficult to get this numb body into my recliner, or in any other chair or couch. Haven't even watched the last episode of "Good Fight" or the late night guys lately, but it doesn't seem to matter anymore, although I could watch on my desktop.

And what use is it to read what passes for news these days? I guess I still have a need to know what's going on in the world, even though it only makes me sad.

What makes me even sadder is that Brenda and I have a habit of watching TV together after supper, and now she's in the den by herself and I'm in what we call the computer room, by myself. I know she'll have to get used to it sooner or later. But ….

So bed will be my option for today, right now. That's about

the only decision I can deal with at present! Just had a half dose of morphine. It would be nice if I don't wake up ....

I hope that something can be done medically for you, Ken, so that you can somewhat enjoy your life and continue to write for us all. Looking forward to your essay on Thursday if I'm still around. Am definitely impressed that you can still do some great pedaling on your exercise bike at times!

Thank you for being with me through this ... it means a lot to me, and I know that you understand totally, at depth. — Love, Bonnie ♥

November 1, 2022
Ken:

Dear Bonnie,

I stopped what I was doing — reading a book manuscript online (which I hate to do) by an old friend with whom I recently reconnected. It's about a swami my friend met and studied with during the 1970s who used music as a tool to engender enlightenment. I've only read the first few chapters, but it's no problem to lay it aside for you, dear friend.

Yes, we live in dark times these days. Even the swami commented that this is the time in the Yoga tradition known as the Kali Yuga — basically, the spiritual pits, an age of endarkenment. You'll be leaving it all behind soon. Where you'll be going there is no darkness. I remember an NDEr telling me that — "There was no night there," he said.

But I can see that you are bored and dismayed at the state of the world, and feel even worse about the state of your body. Nothing to do but wait, just marking time until you leave time and enter eternity. Meanwhile, at least there's morphine to get you through the day. I hope you can rest soon and find some measure of at least temporary oblivion.

It's sad, though, to read that you and Brenda can no longer watch TV together, and that you find yourself isolated more than you would like. I wonder if she could read to you, however, just to do something together and have something to distract you.

As for me, I didn't have a great night's sleep last night, but at least it was better than the previous night. I'm still waiting to shit. I did have to see my dermatologist this morning and got the full freeze-dry treatment of my face. Not the most fun I've ever had. But, all in all, it's been about as good a day as I have had lately. I'm grateful.

Maybe you're sleeping now. Why don't you write me tomorrow, if you feel up to it. There's an old Beatles' song that I'm sure you know that begins, "I want to hold your hand...." I want to hold your hand, Bonnie, and not let it go until you're free. I love you.

November 4, 2022
Bonnie:

Dear Ken — Yes, still here, regrettably ... thanks for checkin' on me. This will be short ... am wearing a rubber glove on my hand in order to type without drowning the keyboard, so there may be some typos floating around. Explanation — my massage thera-pist came here this afternoon ... she is also a death doula and has been visiting me lately ... because, well, you know ... that death thing that is on the horizon.

Today she massaged my swollen, lymphatic legs ... very lightly, legs only. After she left, I started dripping lymph from all over!! Like turning on a hose. It drips from my fingertips and my legs, arms ... everywhere. My son's wife who is an NP ... told us that's sometimes a sign of the body shutting down. Rejoice, Ken! Maybe I'm going to beat you "There!"

What's going on with you ... hope you had a good day, sat in the sunshine (if there was sun there) and enjoyed a good book or music? Yes, we can definitely compare our many woes, can't we? I might have you beat on the lymph dripping though! ☺

Heading for shower now ... so as to mix water with lymph

fluid, I guess. And hope it stops before time to get in bed. I may have to sleep somehow without my bed. ☺

November 5, 2022
Ken:

OMG, all that lymph fluid! You're leaking, gal, but, as you say, maybe despite the mess and discomfort, it may signify that you are starting to head toward the exit, which I know at this point would be a relief. But how are you doing and feeling today, Bonnie? You're welcome to send me an update later if you have time or tomorrow.

Since my focus is on you, I don't want to natter too much about my own troubles, which of course pale into utter insignificance compared to what you're dealing with. Let it suffice just to say I'm tired today and still have my messy shits to deal with. Small beer in the scheme of things when you are having so much to cope with. I'm just so sorry that you never seem to have any relief from the woes of your body, Bonnie.

For now, I just hope that you've been able to stem the lymphatic fluid flow and aren't in too much discomfort today. Anyway, please give me an update when you feel up to it. All my love to you, dear Bonnie.

November 6, 2022
Bonnie:

Dear Ken ... yes, maybe starting toward the end ... very uncomfortable ... heading back to bed now.... Even though my son is on the way here.... He'll just have to wake me up. This is probably not goodbye, Ken, see ya tomorrow ... you get a good sleep and feel better! Love always and deep appreciation. Love, Bonnie. Hold my hand. ♥♥♥

November 7, 2022
Ken:

Are you still hanging on, Bonnie? Thinking of you, still holding your hand. Love, Ken

November 9, 2022
Brenda writes:

Dear Ken,

This is Brenda, Bonnie's daughter. Bonnie peacefully crossed over from her earthly dimension yesterday around 5:00 pm. She enjoyed your friendship, correspondence, and support very much. I want to tell you that I found your messages to mom very touching ... that you were holding her hand. I know she felt that even though it was long distance. May your end journey be as smooth as possible and just know that mom will be holding your hand from the other side. I am sure you and mom will connect on the other side someday!

How I Came to Love an Alien

He had still been a sailor when he met my mother, but he took to her right away, and she, desperate for the security of a stable relationship after my father Phil's long absence and years of unfaithfulness, succumbed to this young, vigorous and enthusiastic he-man. Indeed, Ray Ring was a muscled, tattooed bull of a man, still in his mid-twenties and full of life. To me, however, it was as if an alien creature had suddenly burst into our house with a kind of demonic energy and taken over the lives of my mother and me. I had, without any warning, acquired a stepfather and lost my own father forever at the same time.

Before Ray's entrance into our lives, my mother and I had continued to live with my aunt, uncle and cousin in a fairly roomy house in Oakland where I had in fact grown up. I didn't understand then that it was my uncle George who must have been supporting us since my mother never worked, and that it must have been something of a financial burden to him to have to provide for two families, especially since he was the only breadwinner. Years afterward, my aunt told me that she had seen that it was necessary to induce my still-shy mother to go to service clubs in order to meet eligible men looking to get married, and that's how Ray had met her and where he began to court her in what must have been an ardent fashion for he certainly did love her with great passion in those early years.

In any event, as soon as my mother and stepfather were married in July of 1946—I was now ten—the three of us moved into a very tiny down-at-the-heels dwelling in a depilated court in the same general area where I had grown up near Mills College in Oakland. Another life was beginning for all of us, and the deep bond that had grown up between my mother and me during the war years was sundered at this time by this strange intruder, my stepfather, who was so unlike all the other members of my own family.

Ray was the son of a Jewish mother, Lillian, and an Italian man named Buono, but the marriage didn't last, and Lillian eventually married a man named Ring who became Ray's stepfather. He was essentially a working-class kid when he enlisted in the Seabees during the Depression. He happened to be at Pearl Harbor when it was bombed by the Japanese and had served in the Pacific Theater during the war. Now that he was out of the service, he had to find himself a job and make a life for his suddenly acquired new family. At first, he had a miscellany of jobs—he drove a laundry truck for a while, he became a bus driver, and then he worked as the credit manager in a clothing store. But he had plenty of drive and ambition and was a good provider.

Ray was basically a good man, and was always kind to me—or tried to be—but he also had some characteristics I found it difficult to tolerate. He was very bellicose, dictatorial and full of opinions, which he would bray at us, brooking no opposition. My mother quickly became very submissive to him. I tried my best to accommodate to him, but I had already become somewhat resentful and rebellious. I didn't like the atmosphere in the house, and once my aunt and uncle had moved to another location in the Oakland hills, I spent a great deal of time at their house, particularly with my aunt who had always treated me like her own son. And once I had become interested in classical music, a few years later on, I spent even more time over there since my aunt and uncle had a piano, which, though I never really learned how to play, provided many hours of pleasure for me.

My stepfather was very talented when it came to mechanical matters—he was always fixing things. I thought I should try to learn some of these skills from him, as a way to connect with him, but I was as inept in these areas as he was gifted, and he could see that I wasn't cut out to be his apprentice. I drifted away, probably to his relief. By then—I was now a young teen-ager—I was becoming interested in music and soon developed a passion for it, beginning with opera. But Ray found my singing painful to his ears – "stop that caterwauling," he would bellow -- which increased the tension between us. And he insisted that I go to bed at an absurdly early hour—probably to get rid of me—which I bitterly resented. I did not take well to his ordering me about and did not appreciate how much the giving and taking of orders had been a part of the military discipline that had helped to form his character. I'm sure Ray found be to me an irritating kid, as alien to him as his spirit was to me. He was never cruel, but he could be harsh and overbearing, so in the end, I just tried to avoid him whenever I could and accommodate to him when I couldn't.

Meanwhile, I could see that something was happening to my mother. She had gradually become more withdrawn and seemingly troubled. Of course, my suspicions immediately centered on my stepfather, and eventually, when he was out of the house, my mother started confiding in me, telling me of her unhappiness with him. Although she was not specific, she intimated that her sex life with Ray was deeply unsatisfying. (I later learned from my uncle George that it was virtually non-existent.) She had made a mistake in marrying him, she said, but she could see no way out now. From what my mother had indicated to me, however, although she was always oblique about this too, I knew she had— even then—other suitors and that one of them, a furrier, wanted her to leave her marriage so that they could be together. Naturally, by this time, I encouraged my mother to do exactly that. I wasn't any happier than she in this new family constellation, and I urged her to find a way to break free. But she never had the courage to do it, and this is when I began to lose respect for my mother. She would only complain, but she would never take any action. She was defeated, a captive in a marriage that she thought would save her, but had only confined her to a prison run by a benevolent but completely controlling warden. It was at that point that my mother started her descent into mental illness, which was her only escape.

In time, I made my own escape, as best I could, spending as much time as possible with my friends and other family members, especially my maternal grandfather Bert who lived up in California's historic Mother Lode country in a then small town called Sonora. I would spend the summers with him there and, for a while, also reconnected with my uncle Bill who had moved up there after leaving the Bay Area. With these relatives of my mother, I felt especially at home and could be myself.

～

In December, 1991, as I was preparing to take a trip to Venezuela with my then current lover, Maude, I received an urgent call from California. My stepfather, Ray, had just been discovered to have an advanced and fatal form of cancer and had already been hospitalized. Because my mother was by then old and demented, and because I was her only child, there was no other choice but to cancel my holiday plans with Maude and leave for California as soon as I could purchase my tickets for the flight.

A day after Christmas, I was on my way to the Bay Area to help take care of my mother but chiefly to do whatever my stepfather needed. At that point, it was mainly a matter of filial duty; in the end, it turned out to be a journey of love.

What follows is an edited version of the diary I kept of that visit.

I try to reach my father's physician to find out the latest news concerning his condition.

"Your number, please."

"I'm sorry, I don't have a number, only a name."

"But we need your number."

"Miss, my father is dying in your hospital, and I'm trying to find out if he is still alive."

"What is *his* number?"

Eventually, human contact is made, and his physician calls me back. He is pleasant, but his news is grim. My father's condition is hopeless; he will die soon.

However, he goes on to say that after all, there may be a glimmer of good news, too. On his last visit, he found that my father was lucid – and full of concern, not for himself but for my mother. Indeed, he further tells me that my father's condition had improved sufficiently that he has now been transferred out of CCU and situated in a regular hospital room.

The traffic is terrible, but I get to the hospital a little before 3 p.m.

My father is alone is his room, asleep. He has lost a great of weight and looks old (he is in his early 70s) and haggard. His once muscular biceps are flabby, his tattoos now faded and grayish. His eyes blink open at my touch, but quickly close again.

He is out of it.

I try again a few minutes later. Again a flicker, but no sign of recognition. I leave him a note, telling him I will be back in the morning....

My father is again sleeping when I enter his room at 11 a.m. the next day, but this time he opens his eyes with understanding. He knows that I am there. I hold his hand and with the other rub his arm gently.

"How are you, Pop?"

"Dyin'," he rasps.

"Are you in pain."

"No, no pain."

He has an oxygen tube in his nose and his arms have tiny markings on them, injection wounds and little tubes sticking out of them. He is exhausted, but he can talk. He often coughs, but he will be coherent throughout that day.

Almost immediately he tells me that he loves me, and that he very much loves my mother. Not a day went by, he says, that he didn't tell her that he loves her. He is very concerned about her welfare, and intent on making sure that she will be provided for after his death. He is determined, he tells me with emphasis, to "hang on" until everything has been arranged to his satisfaction. Indeed, he has thought things out very clearly: Who would be paying the bills, what bills need to be paid, arranging for the sale of the house (he still maintains he owns it and had been making regular mortgage payments), the disposition of his other property, the setting up of a trust fund with the proceeds, and where his wife will live after his death – The Jewish Home for the Aged in Oakland.

Through all this discussion, he makes it clear that he is still "the man in charge," and that things will have to be done his way. (My father is dying in character, all right, I think.) In any case, he is throughout all this initial conversation rational, clear-thinking and focused in intent. At the same time, he is emotional and full of feeling, but that seems only to add to the sense of clarity he projects; it does not detract from it. He is still a military man, and he is giving orders. His impending death has changed nothing in his habitual manner apart from strengthening his will still further that he must live until his will is done.

Ray is also very clear about what he wants for himself: To be transferred to a VA hospital for which he has performed a great deal of service and where his friends are. This is his "real home," he tells me, and where he wants to be when he dies.

I am impressed with the strength of my father's will and with the clarity with which he expresses it and his plans for himself and my mother. Because he clearly knows what he wants and what needs to be done, I assure him that I will carry out his "orders" and honor his wishes. When I ask him what else I can do for him, he says there was nothing he needs from me apart from seeing to my mother's care. He doesn't need to have me make any phone calls for him or any special arrangements and there is nothing he needs to "delegate" to me – he will manage his affairs to the end.

But I already know, without asking, what I will be doing for my father. I will be there to hold his hand – he often reaches for mine – and to listen to his confession. His son, the professor, has become his priest. He is sharing from the heart – his grief at his own father's death, his tormented love for my mother and other painful subjects. He cries several times – I have never seen my father cry – and fights back tears at other times during that first visit.

Some deaths need an audience because an audience is crucial for a cathartic expression for the person who is dying and whose drama will end in death. The management of my father's affairs he will leave to others (though he promises to keep me informed and to send me copies of all relevant documents), but for the enactment of my father's drama of dying, I feel I need to be both audience and interlocutor. My father does need me, but there is no need to discuss that; it is silently understood between us. If I can provide any comfort to him, it will be simply to play my self-assigned role in helping him to release as many of his emotional burdens as possible before he can speak no more.

When I return to the hospital the next day, I find my father sitting in a recliner next to his bed. He looks better than the day before though he appears to be in more pain. Most of my two hours with him is devoted to my taking notes in a little pad concerning how he wants his affairs and effects handled – what is to be sold off, given away, what items need repairs, etc. He is also very concerned about my mother and wants me to be sure to note some special things that she needs but that now he will not be able to procure for her – her pills, some shoes she badly needs, and so on. I dutifully notate them all.

Apart from these "business" items, there are some emotional moments. Soon after I arrive, my father breaks down and says that one thing that particularly grieves him, the hardest thing about dying, is that my mother has not visited him in the hospital – not once. I take his hand, sympathize with him, and tell him that I will make sure that she will be there the following day. His gratitude is obvious. It clearly means so much to him to see her again. His love for her is profound and is very moving to me. Despite everything, his devotion to his sick, decrepit and demented wife is immense.

He also takes out his wallet and gives me some photographs that has always kept there – one of me as a youth, another of my daughter, Kathryn, one of my mother, of course, but oddly enough, as I think about it now, none of himself.

He also wants me to have a list of all the organizations to which he belonged and to know of his life of good works. He proudly shows me all his membership cards. This work has been his life. I really had known almost nothing about it – I was never that interested, really – except in general terms, which makes it clear to me that I know so little about this man, and who he really has been all these years. Selfless and giving to his friends and their families, however much he seems to have neglected his own home, which, believe me, he has left in an unholy mess.

The last couple of days he has seemed weaker, his voice barely able to rise above a whisper, and even then, he can only rasp. He continues to give me lists (is there no end to them?) and orders he wants me to carry out, but is also very emotional at times and very loving toward me, an attitude that he only rarely demonstrated during our life together when I was growing up or even after I had become an adult. I kiss his forehead; he reaches for my hand. He tells me every day that he loves me, and I can tell his sentiments are sincere. His feelings all come to the surface.

But he is bored lying in bed and wants to do his paperwork. Meanwhile, he lives for his phone calls and visitors – and he has had plenty of both.

He says today that his doctor has hinted that he might be released on Friday. (But there is no such indication in his doctor's notes. I checked.) But released to where? He is far too weak, so if he is discharged, he is simply going to be sent to die elsewhere. He does not want to go back home despite the fact that I have worked to make sure his bedroom is now completely clean, neat, dusted and polished – probably for the first time ever – and demurs about going to the VA at this time (though later it turns out that arrangements have been made for him to go there....)

The next day, he continues to fret about my mother who refused to come after all when I expected her to, claiming to have the flu. She doesn't. It's a patent excuse and she's simply malingering. I intend to bring her here tomorrow, New Year's Day, even I have to drag her screaming.

I don't think Pop will last more than a couple of weeks.

I have been meeting with and/or talking to more of his vet buddies. In their eyes, Ray is clearly a great man. Several of them have told me "They love the guy." One to them, apparently my father's best friend, has advised me that in recognition of my father's outstanding work, he will posthumously receive a Congressional medal of honor, which will be read into the Congressional Record. In his social service work, my father has without question really distinguished himself and has clearly earned a great deal of gratitude from many people. This work has been of prime importance to my father – apart from the mother it has been his whole life – and I'm glad he knows it will be duly recognized.

When I was cleaning up his room today, I couldn't help noticing that his walls were covered with plaques and citations and various other awards – there must be forty or fifty of them. And there are about a half dozen more that haven't been hung but rest on a table.

I take pride in these accomplishments of my father, which I hadn't truly appreciated – I am seeing a new side of him or at least one that I hadn't seen properly previously. I actually love cleaning his room and feel as though I am paying a kind of homage to my father in doing so. In his own world, he is indeed regarded as an exemplary man, loved by many of his comrades, and he has certainly grown in stature in the eyes of his son.

How ironic, then, that he who is loved by so many only really cares about receiving love from the one person who has always withheld it – my mother. They have been married for 45 years and, according to what Ray tells me, *never once* in all that time has my mother ever explicitly said that she loved him. My father, on the other hand, claims that not a day has passed when he hasn't avowed his love for my mother. Probably an exaggeration, but still, I suspect, a substantially true statement. I don't think I have ever known a man who has for so long and so passionately loved a woman with so little to show for it – 45 years of a tormented unrequited love. What could be sadder – and for both – but my sympathies lie largely with my father. I wonder whether my mother will make one last gesture and come to see him before he dies so he can tell her once more how much he loves her, and perhaps finally hear the words from her that he has waited in vain to be spoken all these years.

1-3-1992. On the first day of the new year there is an extraordinary and entirely unexpected development: My father has rallied and has begun to regain his vigor. He no longer talks of dying or of what is to be done after his death, but of getting out of the hospital and living. He shows no interest in dying whatever or any knack for it; he is now planning to live – for months, possibly for as long as another year.

What has brought about this apparent complete cessation in his progress toward a seemingly fast approaching death?

Probably several factors contributed, but I think the principal one is my mother's visit earlier that day. I have to browbeat her a bit before I succeed in getting her to go in the first place – and I don't tell her in advance this time – but she consents without too much objection and manages to stay with Ray for about ten minutes. I escort her to his room and remain only long enough to see my father extend his arms to embrace his wife.

That visit seems to have buoyed Ray's spirits inestimably, and when I see him later that evening, he is a new man. Or, more accurately, he is more his old self, speaking more strongly and confidently, and starting to plan his future. He thanks me immediately, and with great ardor, for bringing my mother to the hospital and confirms how much it has meant to him.

I spend a long time with him that evening, giving him some of the information he has requested and continuing to take down his requests, mostly concerned with my mother's welfare. His love and seemingly boundless concern for her impresses me once again; for all its dysfuntionality, his is a great and true love, and more poignantly so because so little of it, if any at all, has been reciprocated by my mother.

The next day – my last – with my chores all done, except for seeing the social worker at the hospital, I arrive at my father's room at about 12:30 to find him sitting in a chair eating his lunch with obvious gusto. His voice is loud and strong, even if still a bit raspy.

Sitting in his chair, he is the commander again, the man in charge, both of his own life and that of my mother's. As his lieutenant, I tell him I will see to it that the social worker speaks to him directly about my mother relieving me, at least temporarily, of the responsibility.

My father has obviously always attempted to do good, but

his good works have not been accomplished without leaving a mess all around him, literally and figuratively. The disorder of his home, and especially in his work area, is indeed metaphoric of this. Evidence of his good will and service is abundant, but all of his papers and documents are strewn about, littered with dirt, dust and discarded mail. He has lived his last years in massive, almost inconceivable, physical sloppiness, caring only for what he could accomplish, but not at all for trying to maintain even the appearance of any kind of order. As a result, my father, like an unruly but energetic child, has left a big pile of paper shit on the floor for others to clean up.

Are his expectations of living more than a month realistic or mere fantasy? It is impossible for me to say. He has very low blood pressure now (it tends to be about 85/55) and in addition to his cancer is suffering from congestive heart failure. I have learned – and he knows, too – that his cancer is terminal and has already metastasized from his colon to his liver, clearly a death sentence. He also has had diabetes for years.

None of this seems to matter to him, however, or to deter him from wanting to live as long as possible as well as he can. He says that they are only "nuisances," not obstacles. (Denial can do wonders for the mind.) To buttress his point, he reminds me of previous times when he survived life-threatening illnesses against all expectation, as, for example, when he recovered from a massive heart attack or when he endured the tremendous pain of a kidney stone because of his indomitable will. He also feels he *has to* stay alive in order to take care of my mother. His will to live is of Beethovenian proportions (Beethoven in his middle period, I mean; think of his 5th symphony). He is simply convinced that he can and will live for a while more. What man, indeed even what physician, would dare to gainsay him?

When I take leave of my father, I leave a man utterly different from the one I had encountered only a week earlier. When I first saw him, he could only open his eyes for an instant and without recognizing me. His first word to me, when I asked him how he was doing was simply, "dyin'." But the man I am leaving now is the man I have always known – obstinate, dominating, in control.

Nevertheless, he is different in some ways, too. For one thing, he is full of expressions of love for me. I kiss him often (which I can't remember *ever* having done before), and there is a great deal of affection between us. Before I leave I say – and I mean it – that despite everything I have enjoyed being with him. He replies that "it was our best time together" – and he is right.

During that week, I came to love my father and to see him with new eyes. Thanks to my conversations with him and with his vet buddies I saw with complete clarity that my father's love for my mother was deeper than I had ever imagined and was at the core of his being, and apart from his veterans' work, his personal *raison d'être*. I also realized, fortunately not too late, that his love for me was equally genuine and that despite our radical temperamental differences and my longstanding feeling that he was essentially an alien creature to me with his crude and unsophisticated ways, with his belligerence and volatile temper, that he still had tried to express the only kind of love he was capable of giving. I just never had perceived it that way before.

He had been, I guess, my real father all along, but I had been blind to it, and to him.

But during this week of his seeming impending death and then his improbable if still temporary rebirth, I saw, with increasing wonder, just who Ray Ring was, and my love for him, which for decades had been frozen because of my inability to see him for who he was, was able to thaw and then pour into him – waters of life.

He felt it – I know he did – acknowledged it and drank it in.

How much love I now felt for my father.

Yes, he was right – it was truly our best time together.

And, as it turned out, our last.

∿

My father did live for another couple of months. I had seen him during my Christmas break from the university, and the next time I could travel to California was during our spring break, which came in early March. With two good friends of mine, I went out there to see him since he had been readmitted to the hospital and to help see to my mother's care. We arrived on the 6th of March and stayed that evening with a friend at her home in Montclair.

That morning, I awoke at about 4:30.

A few hours later, I learned that my father had died at just about that time.

I had arrived too late.

I saw him a day or two later when he was laid out in his casket. His face looked noble. I spent some minutes alone talking to him. You can imagine what I told him.

Later I gave a eulogy at a quickly organized memorial service for him. Many of his vet friends were there, and naturally they expressed not only their appreciation to me, but their love and respect for my father. He was just 72 when he died. But at least he died knowing that his son truly loved him, and, for my part, I now cherish his memory after finally getting to know that the man whom I had regarded as an alien for so many years was truly a real father to me all along.

End of Life Revelations

My New NDE Career

I am – or perhaps I should say, I was – a retired NDE researcher. I began my work interviewing NDErs in 1977 and eventually published my first book, *Life at Death,* describing my findings in 1980. I continued my research, lecturing and writing on NDEs until about the time I reached the age of sixty-five around the turn of the millennium. At that point, having authored four more books on NDEs and countless articles on the subject, I accepted a figurative golden handshake for my labors and, having by then returned to my native California, decided to devote myself to life out in the pastures. I figured there were other things I wanted to do, apart from loafing, than continuing to prattle on about NDEs. I was tired of being interviewed by breathless TV hosts who would always be asking me the same questions, such as, "So, Dr. Ring, what is it like to die?" One time, in bored exasperation, I simply slid off my chair. At least that got a laugh.

Anyway, at that point I disconnected as much as possible from my life as an NDE researcher, declined all interviews or invitations to speak at conferences, and began to explore and write about other things that interested me. Some books on classical music, one on the lives of contemporary Palestinians, various memoirs, books of essays, and in the last few years, I took up the blogging life. But eventually since I never was entirely able to distance myself fully from NDEs, I was lured back to the field, at least to the extent of renewing my contact with various NDE researchers and came to know new people who were now devoting their lives to researching and writing about NDEs. Still, I was happy to remain on the sidelines. It's sort of like being a grandfather. One gets all of the pleasures of seeing what others are doing without any of the responsibilities to do anything oneself. After all, when you're in your mid-80s, what the hell *can* you do besides watch tennis and yearn for the promised life to come – at least if you take the implications of NDEs seriously, which I do.

But recently, at loose ends, and wondering what I should do next with what remains of my life, I got an idea. Since I now know and think highly of a number of NDE researchers, some of whom are relatively new contributors to near-death studies, I thought I might be able to perform a service by introducing some of them to you. So I have suddenly become a *soi-disant* NDE researcher booster. In this essay, and perhaps in a few to come, if the good Lord grants me more time on this benighted planet, I would like to introduce you to some of these friends of mine and their works.

But I'll begin with someone who hardly needs an introduction, really, since I suspect many of you are already familiar with his name: Dr. Bruce Greyson, a psychiatrist, who for many years has been on the faculty of the University of the University of Virginia. Even if you're not familiar with Bruce's work, if you read my previous essay about my early life as an NDE researcher, you may remember seeing a photograph of him and me together, locked in a brotherly embrace, because Bruce has been like a brother of mine for many years. He was a part of the original "gang of four" who helped to establish IANDS – The International Association for Near-Death Studies – back in 1981, and not long afterward he assumed the editorship of its flagship journal, *The Journal of Near-Death Studies*, which he edited for the next quarter of a century. In a recent tribute to him, which I wrote on the occasion of a book launch for his long anticipated personal account of his work as a NDE researcher, I expressed my own view of how I had come to regard Bruce:

If any of you have ever edited a journal, you know what a

*selfless and time-consuming task it is. You had to be willing
to sacrifice your own career in order to enable other professionals to publish their own works. That's the kind of
person Bruce was and is. Totally dedicated. And while all
of us in that original group eventually moved away from
involvement with IANDS, only Bruce has remained faithful
to it to this day. In my opinion, no one has done more to
bring professional recognition to the field of near-death
studies than Bruce. I have long held the view that his contributions to the field over more than forty years – his editorship of The Journal of Near-Death Studies, his many
excellent and important research studies, the books he has
co-edited containing his own articles, all the public lectures
he has given, his service to NDErs as a master therapist,
and so much more – mean that Bruce is without doubt the
most important and influential professional in NDE studies.*

His book, which I alluded to, which was published just last
year, is what I really want to call to your attention. In my opinion,
it is must reading for anyone interested in NDEs. It is simply called
*After: A Doctor Explores What Near-Death Experiences Reveal
about Life and Beyond.* And since I have appointed myself a kind
NDE researcher booster, I will permit myself to quote my own
blurb for the book in order to invite you to get ahold of a copy:

In *After*, psychiatrist Bruce Greyson tells the story of his
personal and professional journey from a skeptical scientist to his
becoming the most distinguished and important
authority of near-death experiences (NDEs) in
the field. Drawing on his treasury of forty-five
years of research, and studding his account with
fascinating cases, Greyson provides an always
engrossing and illuminating survey of the basic
findings and implications of NDE studies for the
general reader. In his book, he shows us why he is

regarded as the leading expert to put NDE studies on the map and establish it as a legitimate scientific enterprise. Moreover, he is not afraid to share his insights on spiritual issues that NDE research affords, including the possibility that death isn't a dead end. Both inspiring and deeply personal, this is a book to savor and the culmination and capstone of Greyson's outstanding career.

～

But in the second part of this essay I want to introduce you to someone who, although he, too, has been studying NDEs for more than forty years, deserves to be better known than he is. Meet my good friend who is blessed with a wonderfully delightful and apposite name, David Sunfellow.

David Sunfellow in one of his favorite environments

I say he is a good friend despite the fact that we have actually never met, and indeed these days I seem to have quite a few treasured friends whom I only know from seeing their names in my inbox. But David, if you're not already familiar with him, is somebody you really should know about, especially if you're interested in NDEs. He, too, is now one of the leading authorities on NDEs.

I came across him several years ago when an NDEr of my acquaintance put me onto him and advised me to check out his website (he actually has several – more about those at the end of this essay). I was impressed and was happy to make contact with him. Over the years, he's been kind enough to post a number of my essays, which he reformatted beautifully. The man is an artist (a gifted photographer, among other things) and not just a tekkie.

In this essay, I also want to introduce you to two of David's books. The first one, published in 2019, is entitled *The Purpose of Life: As Revealed By Near-Death Experiences from Around the World.* Filled with numerous extracts from NDErs supplemented by David's own illuminating commentaries, this is a jewel of a book, and ever since it appeared, I have been recommending it to everyone I know who is interested to learn more about NDEs – and this now includes you.

But the book that this essay will be introducing to you was published the following year and is entitled *500 Quotes From Heaven: Life-Changing Quotes That Reveal The Wisdom & Power of Near-Death Experiences.* This book is a bit different from his first because most of the excerpts from NDErs are briefer but they still pack a wallop. I read a draft of the book, and at the time I remember writing David that I really felt that I should re-read it every few years in order to refresh my own spiritual life by re-ab-sorbing the insights and wisdom of NDErs many of whom quoted by David were actually friends of mine or people whom I had myself interviewed.

Recently I decided to order this book to do exactly that. As I told David, my plan was to read at least five quotes a day for a hundred (non-consecutive) days over the next year. After all, although NDEs teach us how we should live and what's import-ant in life, they also help us to feel comfortable with death. And since I am getting ready to leave the building, if not immediately (I hope!), I figured this would also be a good way to prepare myself for my final journey.

Trouble is, I found it difficult to stop at five quotes! Have you ever been able to eat a single peanut and then stop? Of course not, it's impossible. Same with these quotes. And David understood; even he finds them addictive. So I just kept on reading through the beginning section of his book. And now I am going to share some of these quotes with you, just to give you a taste for the spiritual treats you will find in this book.

The best thing to do, frankly, is just for you to buy the book and forget the rest of this essay. But I hope by drawing on it here, it will induce you to buy the book and to share it with others who wish to learn from a recognized authority what NDEs have to teach us.

All I'm going to do here is just to copy out some of the stories with which David begins his book, where he recounts some examples of NDErs who return from their encounter with death with the realization that they've been they've been graced with a sense of total knowledge of the universe. I will begin, however, with a few observations of my own from NDErs I interviewed who had the same experience. And I will continue and conclude by interspersing some further commentaries. My own remarks will be in this font. The excerpts from David's book will be italicized, so you'll easily be able to distinguish my comments from David's quotes. Ready? Here we go....

I don't know how many NDErs I myself have interviewed have told me that during their experience they were given a "download," as it were, of total knowledge, that they suddenly had all their questions about the universe answered, all at once. But I heard such claims often enough to be struck, almost dumb, by them. The mind, at least mine, boggles when trying to grasp what this experience must be like.

I now recall one such incident involving one of my favorite NDErs by the name of Tom Sawyer (yes, his actual name) whom I first met in 1981 and stayed in touch with until his death a few years ago. I wrote a lot about him in my book, *Heading Toward Omega.* Here's just a brief excerpt:

> You realize that you are suddenly in communications with absolute, total knowledge…. You can think of a question … and immediately know the answer to it. And it can be on any question whatsoever. It can be on any subject…. The light will give you the instantaneous correct answer and make you understand it.

Another fellow I knew well, whom David also quotes in his book, had this same experience and told me it was like "being plugged into a cosmic computer."

David, too, quotes a number of such cases in his book. Here are some of his own examples:

> *The Light welcomed me; The Light absorbed me into The Light. So I was part of The Light. Once I was in The Light, I knew everything The Light knew. I knew all about the universe. I knew everything about flowers, plants, asteroids, suns, novas – everything. I didn't have a question for The Light. Why? Because I knew all the answers. I had nothing to ask. I was given total and absolute knowledge about ALL things instantaneously! I marveled in ecstasy that I knew everything about everything there was to know in the universe right then and there. It was incredibly energizing to comprehend all that power, from knowledge about physics, astronomy, psychology, medicine, agriculture, meteorology, chemistry -- EVERYTHING about how the physical and spiritual worlds operate. I felt electrifying elation, being "on top of the world", and so joyful to possess ultimate Truth.*
>
> *I was given total and absolute knowledge about ALL things instantaneously! I marveled in ecstasy that I knew everything about everything there was to know in the*

universe right then and there. It was incredibly energizing to comprehend all that power, from knowledge about physics, astronomy, psychology, medicine, agriculture, meteorology, chemistry -- EVERYTHING about how the physical and spiritual worlds operate. I felt electrifying elation, being "on top of the world", and so joyful to possess ultimate Truth.

I was just there, floating in this pure ecstasy, knowing to the depths of my being everything I had just heard and witnessed. Suddenly, I was being downloaded with information about every question I had ever had. I have always been interested in science, physics, biology, human relations, spirituality, religion, etc. In one instant, I understood all there was to know. I particularly remember understanding all about how electricity works, then physics, then human relationships.

Although most NDErs retain only their memory of this universal knowledge, they typically cannot access it when they return to their body. And yet, some astonishing aftereffects of this experience can and do occur.

For example, Tom Sawyer, who was not well educated and spent his entire working life operating bulldozers and other heavy earth-moving equipment, returned with a prodigious knowledge about quantum physics and well-known physicists such as Max Planck whose name was completely unfamiliar to him previously. (All this is described at length in *Heading Toward Omega.*)

And the man who told me that he felt he had plugged into a cosmic computer, is cited by David in this same context:

[After his NDE] At twenty-six, I started buying books and learning languages. First French, then Spanish. After two semesters, I started on Don Quixote and read Voltaire's Philosophical Letters. Then, I returned to Portuguese [he had previously lived in Brazil]. At twenty-eight, I studied history and philosophy..... I went through most of them.

*They were on history, philosophy, other religions, astron-
omy, physics, and archeology. Excepting masterworks
and classics, I don't read fiction anymore. At twenty-nine,
I began excursions into particle physics and electronics.
At thirty-two, I started designing oscillators and low-noise
amplifiers. One of them is in an orbiting satellite. At thir-
ty-six, I started designing microprocessors. I'm forty-two
now. As a professional programmer, I write about 40,000
lines of C-language a year.*

And other NDErs return with entirely new gifts and abilities,
such as remarkable musical and artistic talents, though that is a
story for another time. For now it is enough to note that when one
is ushered, even temporarily, into the house of death, all knowledge can be revealed that can have a lasting effect on one's life.
Even knowing that can and usually does evoke a sense of wonder
in the rest of us.

These are merely a few illustrative quotes from David's book.
Remember there are 500 of them in all! The book is really a treasury
of NDE wisdom and insights. I can't recommend this book highly
enough to any of you who are drawn to wanting to learn more
about these experiences so as to enhance your own spiritual life.
And it can be yours for the proverbial song. What are you waiting
for?

But if you're not a reader, or even if you are, I have something
else of David's to offer you. You may want to visit a couple of
his websites. Here are two that are particularly relevant to David's
books.

NDE Stories
https://ndestories.org/stories/

Outstanding Near-Death Experiences (YouTube)
https://www.youtube.com/c/OutstandingNearDeathExperi-
ences/videos

~

In some essays to follow, I want to introduce you to more of my NDE researcher friends – new ones whose names most of you probably will be unfamiliar with, but whom you will surely be keen to learn about.

So I begin and hope to continue with my new NDE career to sing the praises of others before returning to watch more of the Australian Open....

Miraculous Returns

We who must die demand a miracle.
— W. H. Auden

You are visiting your eighty-eight-year-old grandmother in her nursing home. For the last ten years she has been suffering from progressive and irreversible Alzheimer's. For the last few years at least, she has been mute, unable to utter a single word, only to grunt at times. Her eyes seem sightless – milky, glassy, vacant. She has no idea who you are and doesn't look at you, even when you hold her withered wrinkled hand. She is absent, just a living corpse strapped into her wheelchair. You wonder if it even makes sense to continue to visit her. What is the point?

It's sad. You remember your grandmother as a vital, playful woman with a wicked sense of humor. In those days, her family meant everything to her. She relished Sunday evenings when the family would gather for its weekly dinner at her home. No more, and not for many years now.

You are about to leave when a movement catches your eye.

Your grandmother is stirring. Her eyes open, seemingly trying to focus. You wait. In a few moments, her eyes clear and she seems to see you. And then – you can hardly believe it! – she begins to speak.

In a weak voice, she says, "I know I've been away for a long time." And then, after a beat, she asks, "And how are you? How are the children?" And she gives their names and asks how old they are now.

For the next half hour, your grandmother reminisces about her family and engages you in conversation. She even cracks a few silly jokes. You are completely astonished, dumbfounded. How can this be happening? Your grandmother is back with her personality fully intact. What is going on? How is this possible, given that her brain is completely defunct, full of plaques and tangles?

After a while, she seems to grow tired, and in a few moments, she appears to be deeply asleep. You leave her then to report to one of the nurses what you have observed. To your surprise, the nurse is not astonished. She simply nods; she has seen this before.

Together you go back to observe your grandmother, still apparently asleep. "No," the nurse says, "she has died."

We now know what has occurred. It now has a name. It is called "terminal lucidity." It has been known for hundreds of years, but until recently it did not have a name. But we know now that, although rare, such seemingly miraculous, if temporary, returns to life in extremely demented people do in fact happen. Such events are as mysterious as they profound and provocative. But recently a number of researchers have begun to study and probe these mysteries, and in this essay you will be meeting some of them, including one who has become the leading investigator in this new field, a man named Alexander Batthyány.

But long before I became aware of him and his work on terminal lucidity (which I will now abbreviate TL), I was friends with an NDEr named Pam Kircher who was a medical doctor and had spent a lot of her time working in a hospice. During a conference where we met one year – it must have been sometime during the 1980s – I remember she told me about such a case involving an elderly demented man who had spontaneously awakened and became lucid shortly before dying. I was struck by her story and thought it was quite marvelous, but didn't pursue it. In any case, for me at that time it was just a one-off event and there was at the time no term for it.

It wasn't until about 2010 when, belatedly, I became aware of some researchers who had already begun to study this phenomenon on the basis both of historical accounts and those of the present day. The investigator who first brought TL to my attention and who coined the term is a German biologist named Michael Nahm who, it turns out, has long been interested in a variety of paranormal or anomalous experiences that seem to defy or at least challenge our conventional ideas of what is possible. In 2009, he published an article about his research, mostly of historical cases, in *The Journal of Near-Death Studies* in which he defined TL as follows:

The (re-)emergence of normal or unusually enhanced mental abilities in dull, unconscious, or mentally ill patients shortly before death, including considerable elevation of mood and spiritual affectation, or the ability to speak in a previously unusual spiritualized and elated manner.

According to Nahm, such experiences had been known for millennia and were mentioned by such historical notables as Hippocrates, Cicero and Plutarch. Even Benjamin Rush, the eighteenth-century physician (and signer of the Declaration of Independence) who wrote the first treatise on mental illness had observed such cases. But nobody thought to give them a name until Nahm despite the fact that quite a few instances of TL had been described by a number of nineteenth and early twentieth century physicians. Nahm's historical research flushed out some eighty cases of TL over a period of 250 years. Here is one such example from that time, which Nahm summarizes. (I draw this account, however, from an article in The Scientific American.)

This extraordinary case [concerns] a young German woman named Anna ("Käthe") Katharina Ehmer, who died in 1922. Her case is especially valuable because it was witnessed by two highly respected and influential local figures:

Wilhem Wittneben, the chief physician at what was then one of the largest insane asylums in Germany (Hephata), and Friedrich Happich, the director of that same institution. Over the years, both Wittneben and Happich relayed the experience many times in speeches and writings, and their independent descriptions of the incident cross-verified each other.

Käthe was among the most profoundly disabled of the patients at the asylum. Happich paints a vivid picture of her mental status. "From birth on," he writes, "she was seriously retarded. She had never learned to speak a single word. She stared for hours on a particular spot, then fidgeted for hours without a break. She gorged her food, fouled herself day and night, uttered an animal-like sound, and slept ... never [taking] notice of her environment even for a second." As if that weren't enough, Käthe suffered several severe meningitis infections over the years that had damaged her cortical brain tissue.

Yet, despite all this, as the woman lay dying (shortly after having her leg amputated from osseous tuberculosis), Wittneben, Happich, and other staff members at the facility gathered in astonishment at her bedside. "Käthe," wrote Happich, "who had never spoken a single word, being entirely mentally disabled from birth on, sang dying songs to herself. Specifically, she sang over and over again, 'Where does the soul find its home, its peace? Peace, peace, heavenly peace!'" For half an hour she sang. Her face, up to then so stultified, was transfigured and spiritualized. Then, she quietly passed away."

When I started to read Nahm's work on TL, I became tremendously excited. I remember thinking that if I had still been able to conduct my own research, I would have been keen to undertake studies of TL myself – because I could see immediately that there was a connected between TL and NDEs. In any case, I had to find out more about this intriguing phenomenon and soon was able to track down an e-mail address for Nahm. Fortunately, he was delighted to hear from me and since his English turned out to be excellent, we quickly began a cordial correspondence that lasted for several years (and was renewed two years ago when Nahm, among several other European researchers, was planning a replication of my work on NDEs on the blind – until COVID quashed that effort, at least for now).

By then, however, I had learned that my longtime friend and colleague, Bruce Greyson, about whom I have written in previous essays, had already made contact with Nahm and had collaborated with him in a new study that drew on modern cases of TL. Here are just a couple of brief summaries of two such cases of people suffering from Alzheimer's disease that they had learned about.

> *The first case concerned an elderly woman who suffered from the illness for 15 years and was cared for by her daughter. The woman was unresponsive for years and showed no sign of recognizing her daughter or anybody else. However, a few minutes before she died, she started a normal conversation with her daughter, an experience for which the daughter was unprepared and which left her utterly confused.*
>
> *The second Alzheimer's case was remarkably similar. In this case it was a woman's grandmother who had neither talked nor reacted to family members for a number of years until the week before she died, when she suddenly started chatting with the granddaughter, asking about the status of various family members and giving her granddaughter advice. Her granddaughter reported that "it was like talking to Rip Van Winkle."*

Synchronistically, I was able to furnish Nahm with still another instance of TL from my own family. During the time I was in touch with Nahm, my daughter Kathryn's mother-in-law died at the age of 98. She had been suffering from dementia for the previous ten years or so. Kathryn, knowing of my interest in TL, sent me the following e-mail sometime after her mother-in-law's death:

The scenario is basically that Bill's [Kathryn's husband] mom, once a highly competent individual, became increasing incompetent over the last few years. The onset was slow, noticeably starting in 2005, beginning with short term memory loss, putting things in strange places & throwing everything away to full-blown advanced dementia resulting in uncontrollable behavior, inability to reason, and inability to function in most ways. She could not sit still, she would wander all day and all night long; we put up baby gates to keep her out of the kitchen, and at night from getting to the rest of the house. She regressed to the mentality of an 18-month-old, and was unable to put sentences together, often saying "I want" or "I need" with nothing else in the sentence. It was rare to get a full sentence out of her most of 2010, and even back in 2009 as we struggled constantly to figure out what she was trying to say. She had dropped from 120 lbs to 82 lbs. At 98, she began falling often, and finally fell on her side and broke her hip. In the emergency room, she was talking in complete sentences sometimes, i.e., "Get me a new leg." That sentence in itself was amazing, but when Bill went out of the room, she turned to me and said, "Give me the bad news." I did, telling her that her hip was broken. She said, "Oh my goodness." She clearly understood. Several times after that, she told us she loved us, not to forget her, and that she won't forget us, all in complete sentences that we hadn't got out of her in months.

We consider it a final gift to us, and although we didn't realize it totally it at the time, she was saying good-bye to us that day. She knew what the broken hip meant; she knew it was the end. They came and gave her morphine, took her into hospice and 3 days later she died.

~

Some years later, I learned that another researcher of some eminence was engaged in a multi-national study of recent cases of TL that promised to set the gold standard for such research. At the time I first made contact with him, in 2019, he was planning to write the first book in English on the subject that I expected would do for TL what Raymond Moody's book, *Life After Life,* had done for NDEs, which was to introduce a worldwide audience to that topic. [I should note, however, that in 2012 Nahm had published a book dealing in part with TL, but it was only available in German.] Naturally, I was eager to learn more so I quickly discovered where to reach him and immediately upon my writing to him, I received a very friendly letter from this man whose identity you will now have guessed. This is how I met Alexander Batthyány.

But imagine my surprise when I read his postscript:

If I may add something personal: Thank you for writing your wonderful books on the NDE, and your contributions in general, also at the beginning of the NDE-movement. I often wondered when a history, or at least a photo book of the early days of the NDE movement around pioneers such as you – will be published, so that those who were not around back then, might at least capture a glimpse of the pioneering spirit of these times. Should this ever be some-thing you'd allow or initiate or agree with, please count me in if I can be of any help. It would be an honour, a service to the history of ideas, and a personal way of paying back a lot of inspiration I owe to you and your work.

Wow, I was thunderstruck! I had no idea that this man had even heard of me, much less that – as it turned out – he had become deeply interested in and knowledgeable about NDEs and knew all about those of us who had begun to develop the field of near-death studies following upon Moody's truly pioneering work. Needless to say, our mutual admiration society began almost immediately and a long series of warm and lively exchanges was soon to follow.

It wasn't long before I learned that Alex, as I will call him here, was a highly regarded and indeed brilliant scholar. Among other things, he had personally known Viktor Frankl, the famous author of the classic book, *Man's Search for Meaning,* which I had used as one of the texts in one of my courses at UCONN. When he sent me his professional resumé, which makes it clear how deeply he has been connected with Frank's work and legacy, I was able quickly to grasp the caliber of the person I was now dealing with and felt privileged to call my friend.

> *Prof. Alexander Batthyány, PhD, holds the Viktor Frankl Chair for Philosophy and Psychology at the International Academy of Philosophy in the Principality of Liechtenstein and is Director of the newly established Research Institute for Theoretical Psychology and Personalist Studies at Pázmány University, Budapest. Since 2012, Batthyány is on the faculty of the Moscow University Institute of Psychoanalysis, Russia where he is on the faculty as Professor for existential psychotherapy. He is Director of the Viktor Frankl Institute and first editor of the 14-volume edition of the Collected Works of Viktor Frankl. Batthyány has published over fifteen books and articles which have been translated into eleven languages. He lectures widely on philosophical and existential psychology, theory of cognitive science, and the psychology of death and dying.*

Alex lives in Vienna, is barely 50 years old, and if I were to give you a full listing of his scholarly work and accomplishments, it would take several more pages. But I trust this will suffice to demonstrate that Alex is a renowned scholar and, as I was soon to learn, a meticulous researcher.

In an article he wrote in collaboration with Bruce Greyson, I had learned about the preliminary findings of his research project, but recently, when we had re-established contact after a gap of a couple of years, he was kind enough to share with me a draft of his forthcoming book. In what follows, and with his permission, I will be drawing on that book to give you a kind of preview of his findings and will then discuss the implications of his work for what they tell us about what happens at the advent of death.

A brief account of Batthyány's research project

To begin with, I can give only a very limited and brief summary here of Alex's findings from the first really extensive research of contemporary cases of TL. His book, however, contains so much more than a report of his research data, but given my space limitations, all I can do is to invite you to read his book, *Threshold: Terminal Lucidity and the Border of Life and Death*, when it is published in September 2023. However, I can tell you that his book is replete with many very moving accounts of TL in addition to his quantitative findings. So let's begin to dig into both aspects of his research.

I learned that, although this was not the immediate impetus for Alex's TL research, when he was a student he had his own TL encounter with a beloved grandmother. But to begin here with an illustrative case that Alex provides at the outset of his book, consider this story, which because of its length I had to abridge somewhat:

My grandmother had suffered from Alzheimer's dementia for several years. In the final stages of her illness, nothing much seemed to remain of the grandmother I knew and loved. At first, she could no longer recognise us. Eventually, she stopped speaking altogether and had to be fed, because she was no longer capable of eating unaided.

On the day 'the miracle' happened, we reached the door, knocked, entered the room – and saw how my grandfather lovingly held my grandmother's hand and, yes, spoke to her! At first, we just didn't trust our eyes and ears. But then my grandmother looked at us one by one (all the five of us). Her large, beautiful eyes were perfectly clear. The haze of oblivion, of apathy, the 'dead gaze' had given way to an expression of limpid vitality. She who hadn't recognised us for a year, who hadn't even reacted when we visited her, addressed every one of us by name. On that day, however, my grandmother said in plain, clear German that she was glad to 'be back', and to see us.

Then she looked lovingly at her husband, my grand-father, and asked us to take good care of him ... She took his hand. I saw my grandfather's face – thick tears were running down his cheeks. Between sobs, he barely managed to say: 'I love you'. And she answered: 'I love you!' – and her gaze ... I myself weep as I write this down, because I can see the clarity, urgency and love her eyes expressed that day as clearly as if I could see them now.

This conversation lasted some 20 or 30 minutes. Then my grandmother lay back and soon fell asleep. When the phone rang the next morning, I knew before picking up, what the ward nurse was going to tell us. My grandmother had died peacefully in her sleep, at the age of 86. It was one of the most beautiful and wondrous and moving things I have witnessed to this day.

There are many such stories in Alex's book, and, collectively, they provide a very rich tapestry of these seemingly miraculous returns to full consciousness prior to death. Altogether, over a period of several years, Alex was able to receive some 214 cases from all over the world – from various countries in Europe, Asia, Africa, the U.S., etc. Respondents – hospice and palliative care nurses, other health care workers, family members – were asked to complete a detailed questionnaire but also to provide written summaries of the TL episodes they had witnessed.

Alex found that TL is definitely a final death-related event with most patients dying shortly after having re-awakened, sometime just a few minutes later but mostly within a couple of days. Moreover, when asked to rate the degree of lucidity of these patients, the overwhelming majority of the 214 participants in the study, 77%, were judged to have spoken clearly and coherently "like normal," and some of the rest were still definitely intelligible. An additional finding of interest is that about a quarter of the patients were observed to show "an increased overall vitality and zest for life," manifesting "increased energy and elation."

As for the length of these TL interactions, they varied from less than ten minutes (18%) to several days, with the plurality of them falling between ten and sixty minutes (42%).

Finally, many respondents said that witnessing a TL in a beloved relative or friend was like receiving a "special gift" (just as my daughter, Kathryn, testified was true for her and her husband) and that they "felt overwhelmingly grateful for being granted an unexpected opportunity to say goodbye." Indeed, the consoling power of these experiences was easy to appreciate from the many such accounts Alex provides.

Implications

By now, you should have a good sense of the nature of TL episodes and the effect they have on witnesses who are lucky enough to have these encounters. But what are we to make of them? How are we to interpret these miraculous returns to life, just prior to death?

In the space I have left, I will just give you my own view and do not mean to imply that Alex would necessarily share it. So I am speaking only for myself here.

The first point I need to make is that TL experiences do not stand alone. They are part of a complex set of experiences that occur with the onset of death. They are clearly related, for example, to near-death experiences, as indeed Alex notes in his book, and what used to be called deathbed visions (now often referred to as "nearing death awareness") when dying people appear to see deceased loved ones coming to greet them, and seemingly offering to provide a kind of "escort service" to the next world. (My friend and NDE researcher, John Audette, playfully refers to them as "the welcoming committee.")

NDEs and deathbed visions, however, are subjective and private, but TL is objective – you can witness it. But clearly with the advent of death mysterious – and thrilling – things begin to happen. The dying person seems to be transitioning into another reality during which the attachment to the body loosens and the limitations of brain-dependent consciousness is weakened and eventually transcended.

At this liminal point, hovering between the worlds, we are preparing to leave the temporal world – and the shackles of the body – and enter eternity, which is not everlasting time but timelessness. All these "intimations of mortality" (to alter Wordsworth's famous phrase) are preparing us to leave this world behind. We are awakening from the dream of life into what NDErs tend to call "true reality." I remember an NDEr saying to me, "I never felt more alive than when I died."

This same man, struggling to find words to describe what it was like to be ushered into this world, told me: "There was nothing *but* love.... it just seemed like the real thing, just to feel this sense of total love in every direction."

Returning to our TL accounts, it is true that only a relatively small minority of dying persons may be observed to have this miraculous experience, but the work on TL implies that *after* we die we all will awaken to find ourselves still alive, with our personalities intact, on the threshold of a love-saturated realm of eternity, our true home.

I personally am very grateful to Alex and other TL researchers (I could not mention them all) who have brought this phenomenon to light and thereby made us aware of yet another remarkable event occurring "at the hour of death" that evokes our sense of wonder and mystery. It was my pleasure to share this information with you and, if you're interested to learn more, to invite you to pursue the topic further once Alex's book is published.

Living It All Over Again:
Lessons of the Life Review and the
Work of Jeff Janssen

A quarter of a century ago, when I was working on my book *Lessons from the Light,* I was particularly concerned to make my readers aware of the profound significance of the one feature of NDEs that I felt was the most important of all – the life review. At least from the standpoint of what we all can learn from NDEs without having to undergo one, the life review (which I will abbreviate from now on as LR) represents the key takeaway lesson from these encounters with death. I ended up writing two chapters on the LR in that book and have always advised people that if they could not manage to read the entire book, to please read at least those two chapters.

At the time I was aware that many people, although they may have heard of NDEs, had only a superficial knowledge of the LR. They might say something like, "Oh, yeah, isn't that when your life flashes before your eyes when you almost drown?" But it is so much more. In the LR, you are actually re-experiencing in real time the scenes from your life and how your actions affected other people, whether you knew them or not. So it's not just that you are *reviewing* your life; you are living it over again, and nothing is left out.

Here is just a sampling of some brief excerpts about this aspect of the LR:

The life review was absolutely everything for the first thirty-three years of my life.... from the first breath of life right through the accident.

It preceded to show me every single event in my twenty-two years of life in a kind of instant three-dimensional panoramic review.... The brightness showed me every second of all those years, in exquisite detail, in what seemed like only a second in time.

My whole life was there, every instant of it.... Everyone and everything I had ever seen and everything that ever happened was there.

I had a total complete clear knowledge of everything that had ever happened in my life – even little minute things that I had forgotten.

My life passed before me.... even things I had forgotten all about. Every single emotion, all the happy times, the sad times, the angry times, the love, the reconciliation – everything was there. Nothing was left out.

But even these excerpts just scratch the surface of the LR. You don't just re-experience and relive your life, you see how everything you thought and felt as well as what you did affected others. Case in point:

Mine was not a review, but a reliving. For me, it was a total reliving of every thought I had ever thought, every word I had ever spoken, and every deed I had ever done,

*plus, the effect of each thought, word and deed on everyone
or anyone who had ever come within my environment or
sphere of influence, whether I knew them or not.... No
detail was left out. No slip of the tongue or slur was missed.
No mistake or accident went unaccounted for. If there is
such a thing as hell, as far as I am concerned, this was hell.*

Before I continue, you might want to take a few deep breaths
and a few moments to let this last excerpt sink in. At least we're
beginning to grasp the enormity of what the LR has to teach us. It's
as if everything in your life has been recorded and during the LR,
it is played back for you, except this time you are able to see how
your thoughts and behavior affected others.

But there's more and now I am coming to the most important
insight that the LR has to teach us. It's not just that you experience, say, how an unkind action has made another person feel, it's
worse than that. And why? Because you *become* that other person
and what you have done to him you experience as an act done to
yourself.

Let me give you just one illustration here from the LR of a
person I knew very well, and I've already referred to him. His
name was Tom Sawyer, and I first came to know him when he
visited me at "the Near-Death Hotel" in 1981 after reading my first
NDE book, *Life at Death.* We became good friends after that, and
we remained in touch for the rest of his life until his death a few
years ago. I wrote a great deal about Tom in my subsequent book,
Heading Toward Omega, but all I will say here is that Tom had a
profound NDE in 1978 during which he had a LR. In what follows,
I will limit myself to recounting just one episode from Tom's LR.
It will be sufficient to make my point.

Here's what I had to say about that incident, although in this
account I did not use Tom's actual name, but just indicated that he
was a friend of mine:

*I have a friend who when growing up was kind of a
roughneck; he had a hot temper; he was always getting
into scrapes. One day he was driving his truck through*

the suburb in the town where he lived and he almost hit a pedestrian. And he got very aggravated with the pedestrian. He was a very big physical guy and a fight ensued. He punched this guy out and left him unconscious on the pavement, got back into his truck, and roared off.

Fifteen years later my friend had his NDE and during it, he had a LR. In his LR, this particular scene of the fight took place again. And he said that, as many people do, he experienced this from a dual aspect. There was a part of him that was almost as if he were high up in a building looking out a window and seeing the fight below. But at the same time he was observing the fight like a spectator, he saw himself in the fight. Except this time, he found himself in the role of the other person. And he felt all 32 blows that he had rained on this person 15 years ago now being inflicted upon himself. He felt his teeth cracking. He felt the blood in his teeth. He felt everything that this other person must have felt at that particular time. This was a complete role reversal; an empathic life review experience.

There's more. Later, Tom went into more detail about what he learned during this experience:

"From the time I stepped out of the truck, I hit that man 32 times. I saw what an enraged Tom Sawyer not only looked like but felt like. I experienced seeing Tom Sawyer's fist come directly into my face. I felt my teeth going through my lower lip. In other words, I was in that man's eyes. I was in that man's body. I experienced the physical pain, the degradation, the embarrassment, the humiliation, and the helplessness in being knocked back like that. I broke his nose and really made a mess of his face. I almost killed that man. He didn't have time to bring his hands up, he fell straight backwards hitting his head on the street...

In the life review, I came to know the man's chronological age: he was 46 years old. I knew that he was in a drunken state and that the rationale behind his desire to drink to oblivion was that he was in a severe state of bereavement for his deceased wife. He turned to alcohol as an escape mechanism for dealing with her death. I experienced unbelievable things about that man that are of a very personal, confidential, and private nature."

In short, Tom had become the other man and not only felt his physical agony, but came to know his inner life and personal sorrows.

This is one of the most important lessons of the LR. You are the very person whom you have hurt and you feel the pain you have inflicted on him. But it's also the case that when you have done a good deed, you experience the blessing of that action because you are now its recipient. And to give you an illustration of this kind of LR, here's one from another person I came to know during the course of my work on NDEs. I'll let Diane Morrissey tell the story herself:

"As the life review continued, I was shown some very special deeds I had performed. [One was when] I saw myself at seventeen, when I'd worked at a convalescent hospital after school. I had grown fond of a toothless old woman who was no longer able to speak clearly, and who never had visitors. She liked to suck on graham crackers before going to bed, but no one wanted to serve her because when she had finished, she would drool as she kissed the entire length of the arm of the person feeding her. While others avoided her, I willingly fed her the cookies she adored, seeing how happy this made her. When that scene was replayed for me, I felt as if every loving spirit in God's kingdom was thanking me in unison. I was amazed that such an act could have meant so much to God—and to me. I felt humbled and very honored. As these scenes were displayed before me, every emotion I had originally felt returned in full force. I also felt as if God and the angelic being were honoring me

for having performed those deeds. I will never forget the love that surrounded me at that moment, or the joy that ran through me. Can you imagine being hugged by God and your angel? It's an experience that defies description!"

We have only begun to explore the LR, but before delving further into the nature and lessons of this feature of NDEs, I want to introduce you to the man who is about to become recognized as the world's leading authority on the LR and who will soon be publishing an entire book on the subject which will contain hundreds of such cases along with his incisive and illuminating commentaries on the LR. Indeed, you will find in his book the very cases I've just discussed – that of Tom Sawyer and Diane Morrissey – and many others some of which I will be citing in the essay to follow. But first, it is now my pleasure to introduce you to this man whom I'm privileged to call my friend, Jeff Janssen.

Jeff Janssen

Although Jeff had written to me more than a decade ago to express appreciation for my NDE work and to tell me that he had already read three of my books on the subject, I had no recollection of that kind note until Jeff recently reminded me of it. In any case, eight years passed before I heard from him again. This time, in 2019, he was writing to let me know that in the intervening years, he had been engaged in a deep study of the literature on NDEs and had just published a book on the subject, which he entitled *10 Life-Changing Lessons from Heaven.* I remember that when I started to peruse and read through Jeff's book, my immediate thought was, "This book is so much better than *Lessons from the Light!*" My book had been an attempt to provide my readers with the knowledge and tools to learn to apply the lessons of the NDE to their own lives, but Jeff's book, written with the same goals in mind, was much better organized than mine and showed how much Jeff had learned about NDEs, and how effectively he could offer that knowledge to his readers. Suffice it to say, I was more than impressed, and ever since I have enthusiastically recommended it, along with David Sunfellow's book, *The Purpose of Life,* as the best books now on the market for anyone who wants to learn about NDEs and how to use that knowledge to inform their own lives.

In his letter to me, Jeff also mentioned that he and his wife would soon be coming out to California and wondered if we could arrange to meet during that time. Naturally, I jumped at the chance and in October of 2019, a few months before COVID struck, we were able to meet at a nearby restaurant where I was to learn a good deal about Jeff's fascinating life. To give you a little background on this man, I will now share at least a little about what I learned about him at the time (and afterward).

Jeff is now 52, but when he was 42, he suddenly began experiencing crushing chest pains, shortness of breath, and pain radiating down his left arm. After nearly suffering a massive and likely fatal heart attack, his doctors discovered a 99% blockage his coronary artery. Fortunately, they caught it just in the nick of time and Jeff survived.

That was Jeff's "wake up call."

At that time, Jeff was a leader in the field of mentoring coaches. Here's just a bit about his work drawn from a website he sent me:

Widely considered the world's top expert on Sports Leadership, Jeff Janssen is the founder and president of the Janssen Sports Leadership Center. Jeff's pioneering work in launching and conducting college athletics' first Leadership Academies with student-athletes and coaches began over a decade ago. His groundbreaking work is what originally started the whole field of sports leadership development and continues to be the gold standard today.

His work in this field led him to most of the big-name universities in this country. I will spare you the list, but you would be familiar with all of these universities and colleges.

But his near-fatal heart attack drastically changed Jeff's life trajectory and quickly led to his immersion in near-death studies. In that connection, he has now spoken with, studied and analyzed more than 3500 NDErs. Aside from Raymond Moody and PHM Atwater, I don't know anyone who has had more contact with NDErs than Jeff.

Anyway, at that meeting, I found Jeff to be warm, personable, humorous and altogether delightful. We hit it off and have been dear friends and colleagues ever since.

At the time, I know we discussed the importance of the LR to which subject Jeff had devoted a portion of his book, but he was intent on a new goal – writing an entire book on the LR to show even more clearly how important it was for people to know about and to learn from. And Jeff has since done that. His new book, just published, is called *Your Life's Ripple Effect,* and having read a draft of it, I can assure you this book can truly change your life, as I made clear in my endorsement of it:

"Jeff Janssen's Your Life's Ripple Effect is the book I have not only been waiting for; it's one I wish I had written! Jeff shows the reader how to learn from the most important feature of near-death experiences, the Life Review, and

does a masterful job drawing out its implications for one's daily life. It is a cliché to say 'this book could change your life', but in this case, it really will once you begin to absorb its lessons. I simply cannot recommend this book strongly enough! Now pick it up and learn how near-death experiences can teach us how to live."

A selfie we took to commemorate our bromance.

If you would like to learn more about Jeff's book and purchase a copy, just go to this link:

https://lifelessonsfromheaven.com/resources/your-lifes-ripple-effect-book/

In my next essay, I will be drawing on some of Jeff's findings and insights from this book about the LR in order to give you a bit of a preview of the treasures it contains.

In the meantime, if I have succeeded at least to whet your appetite to learn more about the LR, here are some of my recommendations for what you might wish to read:

Kenneth Ring: *Lessons from the Light,* chapters 6 and 7.

Jeff Janssen: *10 Life-Changing Lessons from Heaven,* pp. 90-107.

David Sunfellow: *500 Quotes from Heaven,* pp. 56-89.

In my next essay, we will continue to explore further features of the LR. There's so much more to say about it, particularly about the way one's actions ripple across the lives of others, and even the animals, trees and plants in one's environment, which is the chief emphasis in Jeff's new mind-blowing book.

Further Lessons of the Life Review – and Ukraine

I am beginning to write this essay as the war in Ukraine enters its second week. I had considered postponing it, but then I realized that this terrible war will drag on for some time, so like many others who write articles, give speeches or offer sermons, I will simply revise what I had planned to say. Still, it is hard not to think about what is going on in Ukraine. We have all seen the images, some of which like the woman who gave birth in a metro subway or the ancient Russian woman protesting the war with her handmade signs being dragged away by a half dozen sturdy helmeted policemen have become almost iconic.

We are all following the war on our TVs or phones, on Instagram and Tik Tok. It has become both visceral and addictive. We are spared the stench of war, but not its horror. We are spared the sight of dead bodies, but we know thousands have already died and additional thousands have been maimed or otherwise injured. We are spared from hearing the cries and moans of little sick and injured children in hospitals, but we can see them and their weeping mothers. And then there are the millions who are fleeing to other countries not knowing what their futures will be or if they will ever again see their husbands and sons who have stayed in or returned to Ukraine to fight for their homeland.

These images of war mark our days and sometimes haunt our dreams. We are powerless to banish them just as we are powerless to prevent the bloodshed and carnage we are forced to witness. Collectively we weep for the Ukrainians even as we applaud their bravery and resolve.

No need to write more, but I will return with some final thoughts on Ukraine toward the end of this essay after we consider some further lessons of the life review, which we will now begin to explore.

～

A simple act of kindness, like a ripple in a pond,
radiates from the giver throughout eternity.
— Sandra Rogers

In order to examine just a few of the most important lessons stemming from NDE-based testimonies about the life review, I will be drawing on three principal sources. To begin with, I will recount some of my own cases from my book, *Lessons from the Light*. Following those, I will avail myself of accounts from the compilation of NDE quotes provided by David Sunfellow as well as examples from Jeff Janssen's extensive collection in his book, *Your Life's Ripple Effect*.

Here's the first lesson we will focus upon: **What you thought was so important, wasn't!**

Here are just a few samples of this lesson for you to ponder:

You are shown your life – and you do the judging. Had you done what you should do. You think, "Oh, I gave six dollars to someone that didn't have much and that was great of me." That didn't mean a thing. It's the little things – maybe a hurt child that you helped to or just to stop to say hello to a shut-in. Those are the things that are important.

Instantly, my entire life was laid bare and open to this

wonderful presence. "GOD." I felt inside my being his forgiveness for the things in my life I was ashamed of, as though they were not of great importance. I was asked— but there were no words; it was a straight mental instantaneous communication – "what had I done to benefit or advance the human race?" At the same time all my life was presently instantly in front of me and I was shown or made to understand what counted. I am not going into this any further, but, believe me, what I had counted in life as unimportant was my salvation and what I thought was important was nil.

I had a total, complete, clear knowledge of everything that had ever happened in my life ... just everything, which gave me a better understanding of everything at that moment. Everything was so clear.... I realized that there are things that every person is sent to earth to realize and to learn. For instance, to share more love, to be more loving toward one another. To discover that the most important thing is human relationships and love and not materialistic things. And to realize that every single thing that you do in your life is recorded and that even though you pass it by not thinking at the time, it always comes up later. For instance, you may be ... at a stoplight and you're in a hurry and the lady in front of you, when the light turns green doesn't take right off, (she) doesn't notice the light, and you get upset and start honking your horn and telling them to hurry up. Those are the little kind of things that are really important.

David Sunfellow also provides quite a few examples, most of them briefer than the foregoing ones, that stress the same lesson.

In the life review we judge ourselves; no one else does. The Light/God did not. But with no ego left – and no lies – we can't hide from what we have done and feel remorse and shame, especially in the presence of this love and light. Some of the things in life we think of as important don't seem to be so important there.

But some of the insignificant things from the material human perspective are very important spiritually.

I was shown it is not the big things we do in life that make the difference. All the little things we do each day make the difference. Little acts of kindness mean so much to God.

As the Being of Light moved away ... I had gained the knowledge that I could use to correct my life. I could hear the Being's message in my head: "Humans are powerful spiritual beings meant to create good on the Earth. This good isn't usually accomplished in bold actions, but in singular acts of kindness between people. It's the little things that count, because they are more spontaneous and show who you truly are."

One of the greatest light-bulb moments during my experience occurred when I learned "the smallest acts of kindness were immense acts," spiritually speaking. Why? Simply because the ego is not involved in those acts. We do them simply because we are motivated by our inner voice to do them. It is the loving thing to do ... Every day there are countless ways of elevating ourselves to a higher and more Divine Light-embodied soul-being simply by responding to the love within us through doing small acts of kindness.

So it's just the little things we do, the things that we often don't even give a second thought to, that really matter. It's not at all what the world values as important that redounds to one's credit spiritually. Let me give just one more example here that I can testify from my own life really did make a difference to me.

First, let me quote a story from one of Jeff Janssen's cases:

I saw that the love we express ripples out, creating an everlasting beauty that is often unbeknownst to us at the time. I saw this happen when I spoke a heartfelt word, thought a truly kind thought or gave undivided attention to someone.

I recall simple gestures having the most impact, like a spontaneous and genuine smile. For example, I smiled at a woman I passed on the street and it turned her day around. She had been feeling disheartened about life, and my smile changed her interactions later that day with her children and others.

I experienced this same effect one day when I was really down in the dumps, feeling tired, discouraged and in some fair degree of pain. I needed to go to my local market, however, and upon leaving, I happened to glance up and noticed a woman – she turned out to be a food consultant the store had hired – who suddenly flashed a beautiful and radiant smile at me. It struck me like a beam of warm loving light, and it immediately transformed my mood – and made my day. I later met this woman and we became friends. She eventually left the store, but I learned a few years later that she herself had been in a serious accident and had had an NDE.

A smile can change someone's day from gloom to joy. I can vouch for that from my own experience. Think about that when you next encounter someone who looks as if he or she could use a hug. If that's not possible, smile!

Next lesson: **Spontaneous acts of selfless kindness involving nature matter more than you might ever have imagined.**

A few examples follow:

One example of my life review was when I was a little kid. We were traveling by car and stopped somewhere along the way. There was a river not far from the road and I was asked to go and bring some water in a bucket from that river. I went to fill up the bucket; but on my way back, I felt that the bucket was way too heavy for me. I decided to empty some of the water to make the bucket lighter. Instead of emptying the water right there, I noticed a tree that was alone by itself in a dry patch of land. I took the effort to go out of my way to that tree and emptied some of the water at the tree base. I even waited there a few seconds to make sure the water is soaked in the soil and is absorbed. In my life review, I received such an applaud and joy for this simple act that it is unbelievable. It was like all the spirits in the universe were filled with joy from this simple act and were best things I had ever done in my life! This was strange to me, because I didn't think this little act was a big deal and thought I had done much more important and bigger things. However, it was shown to me that what I had done was extremely valuable because I had done it purely from the heart, with absolutely no expectation for my own gain."

I learned about another such case from my invaluable webmaster, Kevin Williams, who had heard it from another dear longtime friend of mine, an NDEr named Kimberly Clark Sharp:

Kimberly Clark Sharp once shared an interesting near-death account of the life review of a woman who saw an event in her life as a child. The lesson the woman learned from her life review is that our actions which seem unimportant can be more important than we can imagine on the other side. When the woman was a little girl, she saw a tiny flower growing almost impossibly out of a crack in the sidewalk. She bent down and cupped the flower and gave it her full unconditional love and attention. When the girl became a woman and had an NDE, during her life review she discovered that it was this incident with the flower that was the most important event of her entire life. The reason was because it was the moment where she expressed her love in a greater, purer, and unconditional manner.

We can see this same effect in actions taken toward another person, too. Here's just one example:

The most important of my actions was an instant I would never have recalled except for the near-death experience ... I had taken a child aside on a very hot day. And this was not a charming or a particularly lovable child. But I wanted this child to feel loved; I wanted this child to feel, really, the love of God that brought him into existence and that brought us all into existence ... I took him aside and gave him something to drink and just spent some time with him ... And that was the greatest of all actions. That filled with me with unspeakable and incomprehensible joy. And it was not an action that anyone noticed. And it was not an action that I even recalled. And it was not an action that I had done with any thought of reward. It was simply an action motivated by love. By selfless love.

And, finally, from our friend, Tom Sawyer:

I loved the appearance of a tree. In my life review I could experience a bit of what the tree experienced in my loving it, two little photons of love and adoration. It was somewhat like the leaves acknowledging my presence. Can a tree experience that? Yes, it can. Don't go kicking trees anymore! You do have that effect on plants. You do have an effect on animals. You do have an effect on the universe. And in your life review you'll be the universe and experience yourself in what you call your lifetime and how it affects the universe.

Again we learn that our spontaneous loving acts in the natural world that we are drawn to express simply to show our care may possibly be among the most important gestures of our lives. What counts in our life review is the love we bestow on everything and everyone we come into contact with – especially when it is done without any expectation of reward or gain. It counts more than you could ever suppose, and you will see how much when you come to have your own life review.

As I've mentioned here and discussed in my previous essay, Jeff Janssen's new book, *Your Life's Ripple Effect,* is replete with cases of the life review that show clearly that we are not single isolated individuals but a part of a huge web of interconnections, not only with other people, but with all of life. Indeed, as Tom Sawyer has told us and as other NDErs attest, everything is alive in our world, whether we realize it or not. So when we act, our actions can ripple through this web, they ramify and can affect others in ways we never knew or suspected – until we have our life review.

We've already begun to see this, but in this section, I want to draw attention to just one facet of this aspect of the life review – how our unkind, thoughtless or even cruel actions can do lasting damage, not just to the individual whom we hurt but to others as well. Truly, we know not what we do when we mistreat others. But we will find out when we have our life review.

Our third lesson: **Think twice before you mistreat others because you will find that what you do will be returned to you with interest.**

> *I saw myself at five years old. It was with my brothers and sisters and my neighborhood friend named Heidi ... He picked up a stick and whacked a beehive and we all took off and ran. Everyone got into the public building, but the last one was Heidi. And I had a devious thought. I said, "I'm going to hold the door and not let Heidi in and see what happens to Heidi." All those bees from that beehive, they stung the daylights out of Heidi. And every single bee sting I felt. I felt every sting. The burning sensation. The swelling. Her mother came to the public building scared and frightened. I felt all her fear. All her fright. All her*

rage. Her father came out there trying to figure out what [happened]. I felt it all. It rippled. I felt every single thing.

The life review continued all the way down to third grade. I was teasing a smaller girl ... calling her names ... she's standing against the wall crying ... And now I'm on the receiving end, meaning I'm her ... And not only am I feeling her sorrow and her pain, but I'm seeing, sensing, and feeling the pain and sorrow in her parents because she's now going to turn out as a shyer and more inward person ... I am also feeling how my actions caused ripples far away, not just in her life, but in her parents' lives, in her whole family, also in everyone around her. So, I really get a full spectrum of the full consequences – all the links in the chain from spending a few minutes in a schoolyard teasing a girl.

I was a 10-year-old boy. I had bullied and mercilessly beaten another boy who was also around my age. He felt tortured and deeply hurt. In my life review, I saw that scene again. The boy was crying in physical and deep emotional pain. As he was walking in the street crying and going back home, he radiated negative energy which affected everything around him and on the path. People, and even birds, trees, and flies, received this negative energy from him, which kept propagating throughout the universe. Even rocks on the side of the street were affected by his pain. I saw that everything is alive and our way of grouping things in categories of "alive" and "not alive" is only from our limited physical point of view. In reality, everything is alive ... When this boy went home to his parents, I saw the impact that seeing him in that state had on his parents. I felt the feeling and pain it created in them and how it affected their behavior from that point forward. I saw that as a result of this action, his parents would be always more worried when their son was away from home or if he was a few minutes late.

Space limitations preclude my expanding on this theme, so I can only encourage those of you who would like to go deeper into this and other aspects of the life review to get ahold of and read Jeff's superlative book. Here's how you can get a copy: https://lifelessonsfromheaven.com/resources/your-lifes-ripple-effect-book/

Right now, however, to conclude this essay, we have to consider some cases that do not just involve kids tormenting other kids but adults who do far worse, even heinous things. Here I'll just provide two examples, but they will serve to make my point.

The first case comes from a book entitled *Whole in One* by my longtime colleague, David Lorimer. David is a distinguished English scholar of consciousness and a leader in the movement to establish a post-materialist science. Here's one relevant story from his book.

[A prisoner found during his life review that a scroll began to unroll before his vision and comments.] And the only pictures on it were the pictures of people I had injured. It seemed there would be no end to it. A vast number of people I knew or had seen. Then there were hundreds I had never seen. These were people who had been indirectly injured by me. The minute history of my long criminal career was thus relived by me, plus all the small injuries I had inflicted unconsciously by my thoughtless words and looks and omissions. Apparently nothing was omitted in this nightmare of injuries, but the most terrifying thing about it was that every pang of suffering I had caused others was now felt by me as the scroll unwound itself.

Perfect justice, is it not? What you do unto others you truly do to yourself. The Golden Rule is not just a precept for moral conduct; it's the way it works.

Dannion Brinkley is a famous NDEr, the author of several books and someone who has had multiple NDEs. Some years ago, there was even a film based on his extraordinary life. I had heard about him for a few years before being able to spend several days with him in 1981 in Aiken, South Carolina, where Dannion then lived. I was not disappointed. He was one of the most memorable characters I was ever to meet in my forty years of NDE research. And we stayed in touch for many years before he passed out of my life.

When he was young, and before he had his first NDE, Danny was in the military. It was during the Vietnam war, though Danny didn't spend much time in Vietnam. He was working as an intelligence officer mostly in Laos and Cambodia. His main job, he tells us in his book, *Saved by the Light,* "was to plan and execute the removal of enemy politicians and military personnel."

Danny was an assassin. His job was to kill people.

One was a North Vietnamese colonel. Danny was able to shoot and kill him. He saw the colonel's head explode and his body crumple to the ground.

Some years later, this scene cropped up during Danny's life review. This is what he had to say about it:

> *I experienced this incident from the perspective of the North Vietnamese colonel.... I felt his confusion at having his head blown off and sadness as he left his body and realized that he would never go home again. Then I felt the rest of the chain reaction – the sad feelings of his family when they realized they would be without their provider.*
>
> *I relived all of my kills in just this fashion. I saw myself make the kill and then I felt its horrible results.*

He goes on to say in a striking and frightening passage:

> *While in Southeast Asia I had seen women and children murdered, entire villages destroyed, for no reason or for the wrong reasons. I had not been involved in these killings,*

but now I had to experience them again, from the point of view not of the executioner, but the executed.

In another incident, he was not able to shoot his intended victim; instead he had to plant explosives in the hotel where this man was staying. The explosion did kill him, but it also took the lives of about fifty other people. Again, this event and its repercussions was played back for Danny in his life review.

... but this time, I was hit by a rush of emotion and information. I felt the stark horror that all of those people felt as they realized that their lives were being snuffed out. I experienced the pain that their families felt when they discovered that they had lost their loved ones in such a tragic way. In many cases I even felt the loss their absence would make in future generations.

Now I want to consider another war and another war criminal. I want to return to the war in Ukraine. I have a thought experiment to suggest to you.

I want you to imagine that Vladimir Putin is lying on his death bed.

Let us further suppose that all we have learned about the life review is true.

Now I'd like you to imagine what kind of life review Vladimir Putin will undergo when he dies.

I will leave you to ponder that.

The Life Review in Reverse

Many studies have shown that after an NDE many people become psychic or claim to be more psychic than they already were. It is not uncommon for them to report various precognitive experiences, for example, in which they see events about to take place. And often they do, just as they had seen in their precognitive vision. For instance, you may remember the Challenger explosion that took place in January, 1986 in which all seven astronauts were killed. I can recall at least three NDErs telling me afterward that they had seen this before it happened.

How is this possible? Well, remember that during an NDE there is no sense of time. NDErs leave the illusory prison of earthbound time and enter the freedom of eternity, which is not everlasting time, but timelessness itself. In short, during their NDE, they have transcended the limitations of earthly time. And given that, it becomes theoretically possible for them to see into the future, and to experience future events in their lives before they happen. But when they do occur it is often with a sense of déjà vu. For instance, as a boy sees the woman he is to marry, he understands that this woman is to be his wife. And when he meets that woman much later in life, he not only recognizes her, but knows he is to marry her. Same with his kids. He has seen them too.

In my work with NDErs, I have encountered quite a few cases of this kind, and so have other researchers. I first discussed them in my book, *Heading Toward Omega,* where I referred to them as *life previews* or *personal flashforwards.* In other words, these are life reviews in reverse. Instead of experiencing scenes that have already taken place in one's life, one gets glimpses of events still to come. This is the topic of this essay, so now let's delve more deeply into this subject before considering a few of these uncanny stories in some detail.

Personal flashforwards (PFs) usually occur within the context of an assessment of one's life during an NDE, although occasionally the PF is experienced as a *subsequent* vision. When it takes place while the individual is undergoing an NDE, it is typically described as an image or vision of the future. It is as though the individual sees something of the whole trajectory of his life, not just past events. The understanding I have of these PFs is that to the NDEr they represent events of a *conditional* future – i.e., if a person chooses to return to life, then these events will ensue. In this sense, from the standpoint of an NDEr, a PF may be likened to a "memory" of future events. For him, however, it is seemingly a part of his "life design" that *will* unfold if he returns to physical life.

In other cases an individual will report awareness of knowledge of a future event after the NDE itself. In some instances, the knowledge will manifest itself (again, usually visually and vividly) shortly after an NDE; in other cases, the individual will recall the knowledge *only when or shortly before the actual event happens.* In such instances (this kind of occurrence has been related to me by several NDErs) it seems the event itself jars the memory of it, bringing back the NDE context in which the original perception was given. At such moments there is usually an uncanny sense of *déjà vu;* the event that had already been experienced is now fulfilled in fact, and its realization is accompanied by the shock of absolutely certain prior knowledge of its outcome.

Some case histories of personal flashforwards

Let me begin with a short case history that was graciously provided to me by my friend and NDE colleague, David Sunfellow, whom I have mentioned in my last two essays.

It concerns a man named Bill McDonald who had a profound NDE at the age of eight when he was in the hospital suffering from multiple health issues so severe that his parents were warned that their child was not likely to survive.

Here is how Bill summarizes what he experienced at the time:

> *I found myself sitting up in this big ball of light. The room was nothing but light, bright light. I was shown things and taken on a journey ... I was shown things, and everything that I learned actually transpired 5, 10, 15, 20, 25, 30, even 50 years plus later. In fact, I was shown a whole panorama of the major events in my life up to the age 59. It only went to age 59. Where I was living, who I was going to marry, the Vietnam war.*

He then goes on to elaborate:

> *I'm seeing all these scenes. The John F. Kennedy assassination, though I didn't know who he was. This was in 1954 or 1955. [Kennedy was killed in November, 1963.] And I was seeing the Vietnam war with battle scenes and helicopters ... I'm seeing my future houses, jobs. I'm seeing my wife. I was eight years old. I hadn't met her yet! [I knew] I'd recognize her, and I did. My wife, I saw my children. I was going out in my life about fifty years. The next fifty years was like a constant déjà vu.*

There were some things he remembered just before they happened. For example, in high school Bill tells his principal that "they are going to kill the President next week. I see it in black and white, just like on a TV screen." He's not taken seriously of course and just told to return to his classroom. But then "And the next week he's killed."

I've investigated other cases that provide much more detail about these life previews. In what follows I will select three from my own research.

A case that will serve to illustrate several of the typical features of these PFs was provided to me by a woman who lives in the Midwest. Please note just how specific were her glimpses of her life to come.

Her near-death crisis resulted from a torn cervix while giving birth to her youngest child in 1959. During her NDE she was met by various beings who conveyed knowledge to her. In particular, she noted:

I learned that there is a time for me to die, and that particular time when I was giving birth was not it. Those beings showed me that if I continued down the path I was on at that time (it seems that I have complete freedom of choice) I would later be living HERE and DOING THIS. I found myself in a place that was not [the town I expected to move to] and all three of our children were grown up. My husband and I had become middle-aged, and the entire scenario went like this:

I was in a kitchen tossing a salad, dressed in a striped seersucker outfit. My hair had streaks of silver in it, my waist had thickened some, but I was still in good shape for an older woman. There was a strong feeling of peace of mind about my bearing, and I was in a joyful mood, laughing with my older daughter as we prepared dinner. The younger daughter (the newborn) had gone somewhere with some other children. This daughter was grown up too, but still there were some small children involved who were not in the picture at the moment (i.e., in 1959). My husband had just come out of the shower and was walking down a hallway wrapping a robe around him. He had put on more weight than I had and his hair was quite silver. Our son was mowing our lawn, but both offspring were only visiting. They didn't live with us.

During this scene was the only time an exception was made

regarding the five physical senses. As I gained the knowledge of what our family would be like in the future, I could see, hear, and smell. Particularly striking was the smell of the salad I was producing (cucumber) mingled with the smell of evergreens growing around the house and the odor of freshly cut grass. Also I could detect my own cologne and soap from the shower my husband had vacated. This picture was only a glimpse, but it made one huge impression on me. I must have vowed right then to never forget it, because I certainly have not.

This correspondent added this intriguing follow-up commentary:

1. We look exactly like that right now (in 1981).

2. Our kids look like that picture too.

3. The rapport in our family is now as I've already described. We have a ball whenever we get together, talking and laughing.

4. Our older daughter has been married, had two daughters of her own, and been divorced. While she was being divorced and making a new life for herself with a job, I've helped her with raising the two small girls by babysitting every day for two years. They are very much a part of our family.

5. Our home here in [the town she lives in] could fit that description too. I only wish I had paid more attention to the way the house was built.

Another case that exemplifies most of the characteristics of finely detailed PFs is this one, sent to me by a correspondent living in the western part of the United States. As a ten-year-old child, in his native England, he was rushed to a hospital and operated on for acute appendicitis (possibly peritonitis – he is not sure).

During the operation he had an NDE during which he had an out-of-body experience (at which time he could see his body) as well as an episode involving telepathic communication with beings who seemed to be clothed in robes.

What makes this individual's experience noteworthy is what happened to him *afterward*. He writes:

After the operation, when convalescing, I was aware that there were some strange memories – and that's what they were – concerning events in my future life. I do not know how they got there … they were just *there* … However, at that time [1941], and indeed until 1968, I simply did not believe them.

His letter goes on to describe five specific "memories" of the future he had been aware of as a child. He claims all of them have actually come about as events in his life, except for the last (which pertains to his age at and circumstances of his death). I shall quote his account of the first two of these flashforwards.

1. *You will be married at age twenty-eight.*
    This was the first of the "memories," and this was perceived as a flat statement – there was no emotion attached to it… And this did indeed happen, even though at [my] twenty-eighth birthday I had yet to meet the person that I was to marry.

2. *You will have two children and, live in the house that you see.*
    By contrast to the prediction, this was felt; perhaps "experienced" is the correct term. I had a vivid memory of sitting in a chair, from which I could see two children playing on the floor in front of me. And I *knew* that I was married, although in this vision there was no indication of who it was that I was married to. Now, a married person knows what it was like to be single, because he or she was once single, and he or she knows what it's like to be married because he or she is married. But it is not possible for a

single person to know what it feels like to be married; in particular, it is *not possible* for a ten-year-old boy to know what it feels like to be married! It is this strange, impossible feeling that I remember so clearly and why this incident remained in my mind. I had a "memory" of something that was not to happen for almost twenty-five years hence! But it was not seeing the future in the conventional sense, it was *experiencing* the future. In this incident the future was *now*.

(He then provides a floor plan of the room he and his children were in and refers to it in what follows.)

In this "experience" I saw directly in front of me, and to the right as indicated. I could not see to the left, but I did know that the person that I was married to was sitting on that side of the room. The children playing on the floor were about four and three years old; the older one had dark hair and was a girl (adopted, as it turned out); the younger one had fair hair, and I thought it was a boy. But as it turns out, they are both girls. And I was also aware that behind the wall...there was something very strange that I did not understand at all. My conscious mind could not grasp it, but I just knew that something different was there.

This "memory" suddenly became present one day in 1968, when I was sitting in the chair, reading a book, and happened to glance over at the children.... I realized that this was the "memory" from 1941! After that I began to realize that there was something to these strange recollections. And the strange object behind the wall was a forced-air heater. These heating units were not – and to the best of my knowledge, are still not – used in England. This was why I could not grasp what it was; it was not in my sphere of knowledge in 1941.

Nevertheless, such apparent memories or intimations of the future are certainly provocative, and it is easy to appreciate the striking effect they must have on an individual when they are later actually confirmed. Nevertheless, a sticky methodological issue must be faced here before we can proceed with our delineation of PFs. Put baldly it is: How do we know these accounts are true? To be sure, there is scant reason to believe that all those persons who report PFs (and who usually aver that many of them were fulfilled) are simply making them up. At the same time, we must recognize that PFs typically have the form of unsubstantiated and unsubstantiable self-reports: A person alleges to have had a vision of a future event and then also claims that the event later took place. Accordingly, we seem to be left in the uncomfortable position of having to acknowledge that such reports sometimes are made but lack the means to determine the truth of the testimony given.

In rare instances, however, a way can be found to circumvent this problem by compiling external corroborative evidence that independently supports the claim made by an NDEr. Fortunately, I have such a case involving a PF that I personally investigated some years ago when I was conducting some research in Georgia. At that time, I was to meet a woman I'll call Belle who had been referred to me by Raymond Moody.

I wound up spending two days with Belle, and I will always be indebted to her, not only because of what she told me about her NDE, but because she introduced me to grits, which were delicious! I was then able to appreciate why many southerners rave about grits!

Anyway, here's what you need to know about Belle besides her culinary skills.

During her NDE she encountered guides who gave her considerable information about the future. What makes her NDE unique and of particular value here is precisely *what* she was shown.

Specifically, she was "shown" a picture of Raymond Moody! She was given his full name and told that she would meet him when "the time was right" to tell him her story.

Belle has lived her entire life in a small southern city, residing since 1971 in a home on a street one block long. Approximately eighteen months after her NDE, Raymond Moody, who was then beginning his medical studies, and his then wife, Louise, moved to the same city where Belle had grown up. To the same street! But since the Moodys lived at the other end of the block, years passed without any meaningful interaction between the Moodys and Belle.

Finally, four years *after* Belle's NDE, on Halloween night of 1975, Louise was preparing to take her elder son, Avery, trick-or-treating. Her husband had asked her, however, not to take him to any home unfamiliar to them. Meanwhile, up the block, Belle, who was feeling poorly, was saying to her husband:

"Look, I placed these things [candies] there for the children when they come around, and no matter how cute you think they are, don't call me because I do not feel well tonight and I do not want to be bothered."

Belle describes what happened next:

"He said OK, and sure enough, someone knocked on the door.... Louise didn't listen to Raymond, [and] Bill [her husband] didn't listen to me, so when the knock came on the door, my husband said, 'Belle, you told me not to call you, but you've got to see this one!' 'Oh, boy,' I said, [and] I got up and went up front. I don't normally ask the children where they are from or who they are because I usually know them, but this one I did not know and I said, 'What's your name, child?' He looked up at me and said, 'I'm Raymond Avery Moody, the third.' Immediately his father appeared in my mind and it says ... now!"

Belle turned at once to Louise and said, "I need to talk with your husband." Louise, somewhat taken aback, apparently replied with words to the effect, "Oh, did you have one of those experiences Raymond is writing about?" Belle – who had no idea who Raymond Moody was but only knew he was the man to whom she was supposed to speak – asked Louise, "What experiences are you referring to?" When Louise said "near-death experiences," Belle said that she reckoned she did, since she had been pronounced dead.

The outcome of this strange encounter was that shortly thereafter Raymond Moody was able to interview Belle, whose NDE is featured in his second book, *Reflections on Life After Life*. Ironically, at the time of their meeting in 1975, Moody's best seller-to-be, *Life After Life*, was still at the printer's, and Belle herself had no idea that she had just met the man whose name was destined to become synonymous with the study of near-death experiences. Furthermore, at the time Louise Moody independently confirmed all the essential details of Belle's reconstruction of this event.

Belle herself concluded her account of this episode with these words:

"It was two days before we got together and this was in November of 1975, and they left in April of 1976. We had become very close and loving friends from that point on. It seemed to be a heck of a waste of time not to have known him from 1971!"

Some implications of personal flashforwards

Personal flashforwards are certainly provocative and puzzling experiences, at least from the standpoint of our conventional understanding of time. But assuming the reports that I and other NDE researchers have unearthed are faithful accounts of people's experiences, we must reckon with them and try to understand them in order to tease out their implications.

Let me begin with one historical account that I believe offers us a significant clue to this mysterious phenomenon.

It comes from the great Swedish scientist and seer, Emanuel Swedenborg. If you read about Swedenborg, you will find that he had many qualities in common with NDErs, including being extremely psychic. Because he was famous, most of his psychic experiences were well documented and verified. He really was able to see into the future.

Many of these stories can be found in Wilson van Dusen's book, *The Presence of Other Worlds,* which is an excellent introduction to Swedenborg's life, work and religious teachings. Here I will just quote one such story which is particularly apposite to PFs. Van Dusen sets the scene this way:

[In February, 1772], John Wesley was preparing for a religious speaking tour and the Reverend Samuel Smith and others were assisting him. The gathering was interrupted by the arrival of a letter that Wesley opened and read with evident astonishment.

Sir,

I have been informed in the world of spirits that you have a strong desire to converse with me; I shall be happy to see you if you will favor me with a visit.

I am, sir, your humble servant,
Emanuel Swedenborg

Wesley told those gentlemen that he did want to see Swedenborg but had told no one of it. He answered Swedenborg, saying that the meeting would have to take place in six months, after his tour. Swedenborg wrote back that he could not meet him at that time, for he was to die on the twenty-ninth of the next month, which, of course, he did.

How did Swedenborg know the exact day he was destined to die? I say "destined" because it seems that he was particularly aware of something that may be true for all of us. Namely, that our lives seem to have some kind of pre-set "design" or life plan, and that when NDErs transcend time, some of them get glimpses of what's in store for them, just as we have seen in the PFs we have reviewed. How the trajectory of our lives are orchestrated in this way – and when (for example, before we are born?) – is something we can only speculate about. But that our future has already been "laid out," at least in its broad outlines, seems quite plausible in the light of these PFs.

Of course, it's not that everything is fixed. It can also be that some things can change depending on the choices we make. There could be, for example, alternative pathways through our lives depending on those decisions, as seem to be suggested by some NDEs I have examined. For example, during some NDEs, a person might be shown what would happen if he chooses to remain in the Light rather than return to his body and physical life.

Here's another way to understand this. Imagine that you, a woman named Sarah, are actually a character in a novel. As that person, you undergo certain experiences. Say, you get pregnant in high school, have an abortion at seventeen, marry at twenty, have several children, divorce at thirty-five, develop breast cancer at forty-seven, and so on. You go through these experiences, but of course, you have no foreknowledge of them.

But now suppose that, for a moment outside of time, you have the perspective of the author. As the author of Sarah's life, you know exactly what she will experience, even if she doesn't. In a PF, it's as if you suddenly see your life from that perspective because you are no longer trapped in time and your little local awareness. What seems to be your future from a limited earthly point of view is understood in an entirely different way when you have transcended the illusion of time. It's then that you can see events that are a part of your destiny, just as Swedenborg was able to know his exact death day.

To conclude, some final brief cautionary tales.

First, don't think that having awareness of future events and psychic experiences generally is necessarily a blessing to be coveted. Often it is the opposite. It can be unwanted, even distressing, foreknowledge. For example, Tom Sawyer was particularly sensitive to impending airplane crashes. He could "see" them before they happened, but he could never be sure just where or when they would occur. What was he supposed to do with this knowledge – call the FAA and tell them that there was to be a crash somewhere, sometime soon? He was actually tormented by this knowledge, and devastated when the crash occurred.

Second, and then there was "the man who knew too much."

I refer to a case that was sent to me about a man who was

shown "the book of his life" during his NDE, but was told he must not look at it. But, like a modern Orpheus, he disobeyed and saw various events in his life that came to pass. He very much regretted having looked at that book; he said it really ruined his life. It was as if he had already lived it and had to go through it all over again. Nietzsche's "eternal return" as hell.

Finally, some NDErs not only have something of a preview of their personal life, but seem to tap into knowledge of the *planet's* future. And what they see tends to be deeply troubling, even frightening. I'm afraid we will have to acquaint ourselves with these prophetic visions in my next essay. What we all are going through now in our world seems to have been foretold in these visions.

The Shape of Things to Come –
According to NDErs

In the fall of 1980, I was thoroughly and undeniably pooped. Late that summer my first book on NDEs, *Life at Death,* was published, and since my publisher had invested a fair amount of money on that book – and me – she wanted to make sure she got her money's worth. So she set up an extensive multi-city book tour that took me away from home and all over the country for the next several weeks. In those days there were quite a few popular talk shows for authors, and I seem to have been on them all – *Good Morning America, The Today Show, Donahue, The David Susskind Show, The Regis Philbin Show*, and various others. In addition, I appeared on any number of call-in radio programs, and was frequently interviewed by print journalists. There were even articles about me and my work in The National Enquirer, which did not please my department chairman.

But at that time stories about NDEs were becoming quite well known, the public seemed to be fascinated by them, and TV producers were eager to court people like me because shows about NDEs were good for ratings. So, frankly, I was a hot ticket and mostly enjoyed my fifteen minutes of minor celebrity.

But when my whirlwind tour was over, I was more than ready to hunker down, spend time with my family again and begin to catch up on the voluminous pile of mail that had accumulated in my absence. Plus, the fall semester was about to start, and I had to begin to prepare my classes.

At that time I was happy to have published my book and receive all that attention, but I couldn't conceive of continuing in that way. I wasn't even sure if I wanted to do any more NDE research. Leave it to others!

But life had other plans for me.

Late that fall, my friend John Audette who had introduced me to Raymond Moody and a few other researchers who had become interested in NDEs came to Storrs, Connecticut, where the university of Connecticut is located. He came to ask me a favor. Would I be willing to take over the fledgling NDE organization he had been running so that he could conduct his own NDE research? I agreed, but only if I could rebrand, expand and rename the organization. Thus was IANDS – The International Association for Near-Death Studies – born. John and Bruce Greyson were very much a part of this undertaking – it wouldn't have happened without their involvement – but it was my responsibility to set it up, recruit volunteers to help me run it, find space for it at the university and oversee its day-to-day operations as well as edit the NDE journal that I had launched. My hands – all four of them – were full to overflowing.

Not long afterward, when John paid another visit to the university, he told me something that really intrigued me. He happened to mention that Raymond Moody had come across some NDErs who claimed to have had visions during their NDES not just of their personal future, but that of the planet.

But what was particularly compelling to me was that these visions apparently were all pretty much the same, as if different people were somehow "tapping into" the same future scenario for the earth. Not only that, but what they were reporting was alarming.

Of course at that time many people were concerned about such things as nuclear war (the cold war was still causing such anxieties) or environmental degradation of various kinds, but what Moody was finding was different – his sample of NDEr visionaries claimed actually to have *seen* the shape of what was to come, and it rattled them. I listened to John's riveting account of some of these visions, and I remember thinking, "Hang it, I've got to look into this." I didn't care how busy I was. I would find a way to check this out.

Nevertheless, I would have to wait a bit. Not only did I have to spend many hours at the helm of the ship of IANDS, but I also had to honor my teaching and other academic obligations. I would have to wait until our spring break when I could get away for a while. But I had already reached out to Raymond to tell him of my interest to talk to some of the NDErs who claimed to have these planetary visions. No one had really begun systematically to investigate and collect such cases, and I was eager to volunteer. Raymond was delighted to furnish me with the names and contact information of a few of these people so come March of 1981, I was off to the south to check them out.

My first stop was to Aiken, South Carolina, where I first met Dannion Brinkley whom I mentioned in a previous essay. After that, I travelled to Georgia where I was able to meet Belle and learn to love grits. But there were others down that way whom Raymond also had put me in touch with. For example, there was a fellow named Andy who, like Dannion, had had an NDE as a result of being struck by lightning. He was less fortunate than Dannion, however, losing an arm and having to use a wheelchair. Andy was another fascinating character, however. He was uneducated, but he came back with a thirst for knowledge, as other NDErs often report. And he, too, had been given a vision of the earth's future. I really liked this guy and his girlfriend whose name I never learned but whom he called "Snow White." Snow White, a coy and fetching blonde, seemed to subsist mainly on sugar cubes and Coca-Cola (remember I was in Georgia, the birthplace of Coca-Cola). There were times when I felt I had walked into Erskine Caldwell's *God's Little Acre* and was meeting characters from that novel. Honestly, I had a ball on that trip to the south; everyone I met had enchanted me.

But I was also learning a lot about these planetary visions, and they were the opposite of enchanting. We will get to that soon.

In any event, after that excursion I was to find quite a few other people who had had planetary visions, some of whom I was able to interview. But when I couldn't arrange to see them, I could still gather relevant information through phone calls, cassette tapes and correspondence. By the end of the year, I had managed to locate sixteen people who were able to describe for me their vision of the planet's future.

Over the next few years, I continued to find several more such accounts and by 1988, I had about two dozen in my collection. Meanwhile, some other researchers were following my lead. An English researcher I knew, Margot Grey, reported a few more in 1984, and her findings were virtually identical to mine. More recently, several other researchers have also collected and collated such cases and all of them likewise have confirmed my initial findings. We all were hearing the same stories. If you'd like to look into these more recent studies, you may wish to download an ebook from by Robert and Suzanne Mays based on their 2019 presentation entitled "Prophetic Visions in Near-Death Experiences: Warnings For Our Times." There is also an excellent compilation and commentary on these cases by my webmaster, Kevin Williams, on his website that can be found here: https://near-death.com/future/ And while you're at it, you may also want to visit Kevin's splendid website itself, which has loads of fascinating content. You can check it out at https://near-death.com/.

In my own publications on this topic, I have generally used the generic term prophetic visions (PVs) when discussing these experiences and I will use that terminology for the remainder of this blog. So what have we learned about PVs?

To begin with, PVs differ from PFs (personal flashforwards) in two principal ways: (1) PVs refer to future events that have a global rather than a personal focus; and (2) they are highly consistent from person to person. This latter characteristic makes them especially remarkable. That is, just as NDEs mostly seem to reflect a prototypical pattern, first identified by Raymond Moody, so do PVs. Indeed, I personally have not found a single exception to this general pattern of PVs, which I will delineate in a moment, nor, to my knowledge, have other researchers. It is not just this overall consistency, however, that makes PVs so compelling. Rather, it is their specific apocalyptic *content* that arrests our attention as well as arousing our anxieties about the future.

So, finally, what is the general scenario that is recounted by people who experience these PVs?

I have already indicated that the broad outlines of PVs are much the same for different individuals. Indeed, PVs – as an aspect of NDEs – are analogous to NDEs as a whole in the sense that though no two are identical, the elements that comprise them occur again and again and form a coherent pattern. Here now is a succinct delineation of that pattern:

There is, first of all, a sense of having total knowledge, but specifically one is aware of seeing the entirety of the earth's evolution and history from the beginning to the end of time. The future scenario, however, is usually of short duration, seldom extending much beyond the beginning of the twenty-first century. The individuals report that during this period there will be an increasing incidence of earthquakes, volcanic activity, and generally massive geophysical changes. There will be resultant disturbances in weather patterns and food supplies. The world economic system will collapse, and the possibility of nuclear war or accident is very great (respondents are not agreed on whether a nuclear catastrophe will occur). All of these events are transitional rather than ultimate, however, and they will be followed by a new era in human history marked by human brotherhood, universal, love, and world peace. Though many will die, the earth will live. While agreeing that the dates for these events are not fixed, most individuals felt that they were likely to take place during the 1980s, particularly around the year 1988.

To give one specific example, here's a brief summary from one of Margot Grey's respondents:

*There are going to be a lot of upheavals such as earth-
quakes and volcanoes occurring in the next few years,
which are going to get increasingly worse. I was given to
understand that these activities are a reflection of all the
social upheaval and violence that is going on all over the
world at the moment.*

*Among the many volcanic eruptions that are going to
occur, I saw the one that just occurred in Hawaii. As I saw
the pictures on the television, it was really quite uncanny,
as I had already seen it taking place during the vision I had
seen at the time of my NDE.*

*There are going to be serious food shortages around
the world due to droughts in many places. This will push
the price of food up so that many people will have to
start going without things that they have always taken for
granted.*

*There are going to be very severe droughts in many
countries. Others are going to suffer from freak storms that
will cause tidal waves or flooding to happen as a result
of unnaturally heavy rainfall ... All in all, the weather is
going to be very unpredictable from now on, in fact these
disturbances in the weather patterns have already started.*

This PV was reported during the 1980s, almost forty years ago,
but it easily could have come today from watching the weather
reports on your favorite network's daily news program. That's
what makes these PVs seem so eerily prescient.

Here are a few more brief comments from my own sample of
PV cases that also seem to reflect what is currently happening in
our world. The geophysical changes they report would naturally
be expected to bring about a host of meteorological disruptions in
their wake. These changes, too, have been glimpsed by near-death
survivors who report PVs.

*Oh, my God, that's going to be terrible. The weather is
going to go crazy. We're just as likely to have snow in the*

middle of the summer as one-hundred-degree weather.... I
see droughts in other countries.

I think around 1984, 1985, possibly even sooner, [we'll
see] the beginnings of droughts. I guess we are even suffer-
ing some of that now [1980].

Such drastic changes in the world's physical state will
necessarily disrupt commerce and, indeed, every aspect of
global life. Famine, social disorder, and economic collapse
will be the result.

Here is just one brief summary by one of my respondents of
these foreseen effects:

We'll start getting more droughts, which will bring about
shortages in crops, and the shortage in crops will cause
food prices to rise, which will cause a strain on the
economic situation, which is already going downhill. Also,
at the same time ... because of the shortage of food and
the failing economy, I see a strengthening of arms, which
causes tension ... These kinds of hostilities and [increas-
ing] inflation start more hostilities.

And to amplify this last point and bring it to bear on what is
happening today in Ukraine, this is what Dannion Brinkley had to
say forty years ago:

Watch the Soviet Union. How the Russian people go, so
goes the world. What happens to Russia is the basis for
everything that will happen to the economy of the free
world.

Before we tackle the possible significance of these PVs for our
own time, there is one more facet of these PVs I need to discuss.

One really fascinating aspect of my research on PVs – and
Margot Grey found the same thing in her study – is that many
of the reports we were given tended to focus on one single year,

1988, when a lot of these catastrophic effects would culminate. Even George Ritchie who had his NDE in 1943 made a point of mentioning the year 1988, which obviously was forty-five years in the future at that time. One has to wonder why so many of these PVs tended to converge on this particular year. What *was* it about that year, 1988?

I happen to remember it well. That summer I drove across the country from Connecticut to Colorado with my then wife, Barbara, who had taught for ten years at the University of Colorado, which is located in Boulder. We spent the summer there, often hiking in the Flatirons around the city. It was uncommonly hot that summer, and I remember on our way home, in our non-air-conditioned car, how beastly and oppressively hot it was. Everybody was taking about the heat that summer. And, incidentally it was that same year that James Hansen, the now famous climate scientist, first warned us (and Congress) of the dangers of what was then called "global warming." I also remember reading an article a few years later that presented evidence that there was in fact an unusual amount of volcanic and other geological activity that year.

Had Margot's and my PV experiencers somehow been able to "tap into" these portentous weather-related disruptions – clearly the precursors of things to come that have now arrived in our own time like one of the avenging horsemen of the apocalypse?

Of course, the worst of these PV prophecies did not manifest in 1988, but, still, that year did seem to mark the beginning of our dawning awareness of the perils of climate change. Did we somehow manage to "dodge a bullet" that year, only to have it come speeding our way in the decades since?

After all, as Kevin Williams astutely points out in his 2019 article on the subject:

A successful apocalyptic prophecy is one that doesn't happen.

The goal of apocalyptic prophecy is to warn people to prevent it from happening. The reason prophecies are given to humanity is to change current trends and change enough people so that the prophecy will be diverted. Well-known prophecies that were foretold to occur around the millennium have not happened. Skeptics point out that this proves these prophecies to be false, but .... because the prophecy gives an exact date, the prophecy may still be valid and the date may be wrong.

This is an important point. Remember how much emphasis I have already given to the fact that in NDEs there is no time. There is no real way to accurately translate into an earthly time frame events that appear to a person undergoing an NDE or a PV. So it is at least possible that the persons I interviewed back in the early 1980s were truly tuned into the shape of things to come, but had been in error about when they would manifest. From everything I have presented in this essay, there is an almost inescapable presentiment that that time is – now.

But hold on. Let's pause the talk of earthly doom and destruction for a moment. We still haven't discussed what to make of these experiences. In my book, *Heading Toward Omega,* and in some of the articles I've written on this topic, I consider a range of interpretative possibilities for these PVs. For those, I will have to refer you to my book; we don't have the space for such an extended discussion here. Instead, I will just offer a few final points for your consideration and possible subsequent rumination.

First, many, if not all, persons who have experienced a PV are agreed that our planetary future is not absolutely fixed. (Kevin Williams provides many such examples of this view.) PVs have the form, if x continues, then y is likely, but if x changes, so does y. Planetary cataclysm isn't fated to occur; it can still be averted. Our current dark time doesn't necessarily have to turn to black.

Second, when I first was researching this topic, I myself did not take these PVs literally. I thought there were other ways that they could be understood. The fact that these people were agreed on the globally cataclysmic events that they foresaw in their visions certainly had to be acknowledged and confronted, but I could not persuade myself that we were locked into some kind of doomsday scenario. And I still can't.

To be sure, the future of our planet now does not look inviting. How many of us who have a chance to live until the year 2050, say (count me out; I will be long gone by then), look forward to life on an increasingly, perhaps unbearably, hot planet then?

Nevertheless, individually and collectively, we human beings have agency. We do not have to be fatalistic and passive about the future. We can – and we must – take action to spare our dear and precious earth from the peril it now is in. So I suggest that we take these PVs as warnings, not as forecasts of something inevitable. The fate of the earth may now be threatened by disaster, but if we have the will and the courage, we can still change the shape of things to come.

About the Author

Kenneth Ring, Ph.D, is Professor Emeritus of Psychology at the University of Connecticut, the author of five books dealing with near-death experiences (NDEs) including *Lessons from the Light,* and the co-founder and Past President of The International Association for Near-Death Studies (IANDS).

He currently lives in California, and at 87, he is hopeful that this will be his last book but not a posthumous one.

Here he is in a recent photo with his daughter, Kathryn.